THE
PARENTS'
DIRECTORY

BEDFORD SQUARE PRESS

Bedford Square Press is the publishing imprint of the National Council for Voluntary Organisations. It publishes books on a wide range of current social issues. Series published so far include Survival Handbooks, Community Action, Practical Guides, Directories, Reports, Organisation and Management, and Fundraising.

If you would like to receive a copy of the latest Bedford Square Press catalogue, please write to:

> Sales Manager
> Bedford Square Press
> 26 Bedford Square
> London WC1B 3HU

NATIONAL COUNCIL FOR VOLUNTARY ORGANISATIONS

The National Council for Voluntary Organisations is the leading voluntary agency for the maintenance and promotion of voluntary social action. Its aims are to extend the involvement of voluntary organisations in responding to social issues; to protect the interests and independence of such organisations; and to act as a resource centre providing information, training, legal, publishing and advisory services for the voluntary sector. It also works to develop co-operation between voluntary organisations and statutory authorities, and to encourage international co-operation in voluntary and social service.

THE
PARENTS'
DIRECTORY

Compiled by Fiona Macdonald
With a Foreword by Esther Rantzen

BEDFORD SQUARE PRESS

Published by
BEDFORD SQUARE PRESS of the
National Council for Voluntary Organisations
26 Bedford Square, London WC1B 3HU
© NCVO 1989

Typeset by The Wordshop
The Old Town Hall, Bury Road
Haslingden, Rossendale

Printed and bound in England by
J.W. Arrowsmith Ltd, Bristol

Cover printed by the Heyford Press,
Northampton

British Library Cataloguing in Publication Data
Macdonald, Fiona
    The parents' directory.
    1. Great Britain. Voluntary welfare services,
    – Directories
    I. Title
    361.7′025′41
    ISBN 0–7199–1235–0

Contents

Foreword

When you become a parent, as every parent knows, everything
in your life changes; nothing can be the same again.   There
is no delight like your own child's happiness, no pain as great
as your child's misery.   Rationally you know you will never be
able to defend your child from every danger, but the thought
that your children could be threatened, could be suffering,
rouses you to fight with all your strength to protect them.

There are moments of uncertainty in every parent's life.
Fortunately, in today's world there are also many kinds of help,
advice and support on offer.   Whatever the problem involving
a child's health or handicap, education or leisure, there is
bound to be an organisation that can offer a helping hand.
You only need to spend a few minutes glancing through the pages
of The Parents' Directory to see what an astonishing variety
of voluntary bodies there are for parents to turn to.

Many of these organisations, both old and new, have been
set up by parents themselves.   They are run by people who have
direct experience of a particular problem and so they offer
easy access to parents seeking help.   Some were started by an
individual or a small group who have found a gap in the existing
support structure, and have decided to fill it themselves.
One of the many virtues of this book is that it tells you where
to go for information if you want to set up your own group.

If parenthood is the exploration of a new, exciting and
challenging world, The Parents' Directory provides an excellent
and comprehensive map.   I believe parents will benefit from
it but, most importantly, their children will benefit even more.

Esther Rantzen

Preface

This directory lists about 800 voluntary
organisations which can offer help, advice
and information to parents on a wide range of
topics. We hope that it will enable parents
with problems, or parents in search of
information, to find out about organisations
which can do something positive to meet their
needs. We hope, too, that it will enable
parents and children with similar interests or
concerns to make contact with one another
through local branches of voluntary
organisations, and find friendship, support
and encouragement.

For reasons of space, this directory lists
only a proportion of the large number of
voluntary organisations which exist to help
parents and children. We hope we have
included a useful and representative
selection, but we are always glad to hear of
existing organisations which we have
omitted, or of new organisations formed since
the directory was published. If you would like
your organisation to be considered for
inclusion in the next edition of this directory,
please complete the form on page 115.

The publishers wish to acknowledge the
following individuals and organisations for
their help in preparing this edition of *The
Parents' Directory*:

Research and co-ordination Fiona Macdonald
Administration Anne Pollard
Index Nesta Evans
Additional material Jane Grant, Jacqueline
Sallon

How to use the directory

This directory is divided into five main subject categories, dealing with Education, Family Welfare, Handicap, Health and Leisure. Each of these subject categories is subdivided into a number of more specialised sub-sections; you can see how these are arranged by looking at the contents list. Organisations are listed in alphabetical order within each sub-section. Some organisations provide information or services relevant to more than one main subject category; they are described in full once, and then cross-referenced.

Each organisation is described according to a standard pattern:

Name
Address
Telephone number
Person to contact
Brief description of aims and activities
Symbols to give further information, as appropriate:

    C = a registered charity
    B = has branches or local groups
    V = volunteers welcomed
    P = produces publications

Criteria for inclusion

The organisations listed in this directory are all 'voluntary agencies' – that is, self-governing groups of people who have joined together voluntarily to take action for the betterment of the community. Organisations affiliated to any political party are not included, nor are organisations set up primarily for financial gain. The appearance of an entry describing an organisation and its activities should not be taken to mean that NCVO endorses that organisation.

Most of the organisations listed are dependent on voluntary fund-raising, occasionally supplemented by grants from central or local government. Entries have been restricted to those organisations which are countrywide in character, or which are regarded as leading bodies in their field, or which welcome enquiries from anywhere in the country. Similar organisations which function exclusively in Scotland, Wales or Northern Ireland have not been included; you can find out about them from the 'umbrella' organisations listed on page 104.

Accuracy of contents

The publishers cannot accept responsibility for statements made in the directory section. The entries are based on information supplied or checked by the organisations concerned, edited where necessary to standardise presentation. While every effort has been made to ensure details are accurate and up-to-date, some changes in contact names or addresses may have occurred between going to press and date of publication.

EDUCATION

GENERAL ORGANISATIONS

British Association for Early Childhood Education

111 City View House, 463 Bethnal Green Road, London N2 9QH
01–739 7594
Contact B Boon
Provides information and publishes a wide range of materials on the development of children aged 0 – 9 years. Holds conferences, meetings and seminars. Membership open to all.
C B V P

Education Alliance

Congress House, Great Russell Street, London WC1B 3LS
01–636 4030 ext 172
Contact Amanda Wood
A non-partisan, umbrella organisation seeking to bring together all those interested in education.
C B V P

Girls' Public Day School Trust

20 Queen Anne's Gate, London SW1H 9AN
01–222 9595
Runs 25 independent schools for girls, which provide education of a high academic standard at relatively low fees. Assisted places and bursaries are available.
C P

Home and School Council

81 Rustlings Road, Sheffield S11 7AB
0742–662467
Contact Barbara Bullivant
Co-ordinates national parents' organisations; produces publications on home-school relations.
V P

International Friendship League

Peace Haven, 3 Creswick Road, London W3 9HE
01–992 0221
Contact Babs Macdonald
A voluntary, non-commercial and non-political organisation open to all people of all races and religious opinions. Provides hospitality to overseas visitors; organises social and educational activities for members, including junior members.
B C P

National Association of Governors and Managers

81 Rustlings Road, Sheffield S11 7AB
0742–662467
Contact Barbara Bullivant
Aims to improve school government, to develop school-community links, to widen membership of school governing bodies and to extend their powers. Provides training for governors.
V P

National Confederation of Parent Teacher Associations

43 Stonebridge Road, Northfleet, Gravesend, Kent DA11 9DS
0474–60618
Contact Sheila Naybour
Aims to encourage good relationships and co-operation between home and school. Gives advice and assistance to any group wishing to set up a PTA.
C B V P

National Federation of Community Organisations

8–9 Upper Street, London N1 0PQ
Contact Diana Hopkins
Promotes the activities of community associations in the areas of education, recreation, leisure and social welfare. Can provide information and advice.
C B V P

National Organisation for Initiatives in Social Education

Bayswater Centre, 15/17 Bayswater Avenue, Redland, Bristol BS6 7NU
0272–741995
Contact Christine Gray
Promotes 'social education' (initiatives for encouraging young people to work to improve their own lives and benefit the world around them). Runs an information service, and training courses for those who work with young people.
B V P

Pre-School Playgroups Association

Alford House, Aveline Street, London SE11 5DH
01–582 8871
Encourages the formation of playgroups and mother and toddler groups, and the active involvement of parents in providing them. Maintains a network of voluntary organisers and local branches.
C B V

Quaker Social Responsibility and Education

see under FAMILY WELFARE, p.27

ADVICE AND INFORMATION

Advisory Centre for Education

18 Victoria Park Square, London E2 9PB
01–980 4596
Contact Information Workers

Provides a free advice service for parents of children in state-maintained schools. Campaigns to make state schools more responsive to the needs of parents and children.
C P

Aids to Communication in Education

Ormerod School, Waynflete Road, Headington, Oxford OX3 8DD
0865–63508
Contact Andrew Lysey
Provides information on communication aids to parents, teachers and therapists; runs a centre where children's needs may be assessed, and the effectiveness of a wide variety of communication aids investigated and evaluated.
C P

Association for Behavioural Approaches with Children

4 The Stables, Old Birmingham Road, Alvechurch, Worcs B48 7TQ
021–445 5482
Contact Susan Colmar
A multi-disciplinary organisation which aims to provide support services to all those interested in, or already using, behavioural techniques in their work with children. Members include teachers, social workers, psychologists, researchers and parents.
B P

Association for the Study of the Curriculum

Forest Lodge School, Lodge Lane, College Row, Romford, Essex RM5 2LD
0708–464213
Contact Rod Piper
Holds meetings and produces publications for all people interested in the curriculum.
C B V P

Centre for the Study of Comprehensive Schools

Wentworth College, University of York, Heslington, York YO1 5DD
0904–433240
Contact Liza Griffiths
A national organisation for all who have an interest in the quality of education received by the 90% of children who attend comprehensive schools. Maintains information database; publishes a broadsheet on parent-school partnership.
C P

CETU (Non-Formal Education) Ltd

124 Lord Street, Halifax, West Yorks
0422–57394
Contact Pat McGeever
Largely an adult education organisation, encouraging people to make better use of their own learning potential and to help the community, but may be able to supply information about people with particular skills and an interest in informal education for all ages in your area.
C B V P

Education Otherwise

25 Common Lane, Hemingford Abbots, Cambridgeshire PE18 9AN
0480–63130
Contact Janet Everdell
Offers support, advice and information to parents practising or contemplating home-based education as an alternative to schooling.
B P

Educational Centres Association

Chequer Centre, Chequer Street, London EC1Y 8PL
01–251 4158
Contact Dominic Delahunt
Represents mature adult education students and professionals in a wide range of educational institutions.
C B V P

Federation of Children's Book Groups

5 West Way, Broadstone, Dorset BH18 9LW
0202–695929
Contact Pat Clark
Promotes an interest in children's literature, principally among parents, and encourages the wider distribution and availability of books for children.

Forum for the Advancement of Educational Therapy

3 Templewood, Ealing, London W13 8BA
01–998 4224
Contact Gerda Hanko
Largely a professional association of therapists concerned to promote an understanding of the importance of emotional factors in learning and failure to learn. May be able to refer parents to therapists in their area.
C B V P

Independent Panel of Special Education Experts

12 Marsh Road, Tillingham, Essex CM0 7SZ
0621–87781
Contact John Wright
Aims to provide parents with free, expert second opinions on their children's special educational needs from a panel of volunteer professionals, all of whom are qualified, experienced, and currently working in special education.
C V

Independent Schools Information Service

56 Buckingham Gate, London SW1E 6AG
01–630 8793/4
Provides information, advice and help to parents on choosing an independent school. Publishes annual guide and information leaflets. Runs international service for overseas

parents. Runs parents' supporters club – ISIS Association.
B V P

Inter-Action Trust
HMS President (1980), Victoria Embankment, London EC4Y 0HZ
01–583 2652
Contact Erica Lander
Offers advice and consultancy on the setting up of creative learning programmes/activities for young people and those who care for them.
C V P

Intercultural Exchange Programmes
Seymour Mews House, Seymour Mews, London W1H 9PE
01–486 5462
Aims to promote international understanding through a programme of educational exchanges for 16–18 year olds.
C B V

International Association of Educational and Vocational Guidance
c/o Gloucester House, Chichester Street, Belfast BT1 7RA
0232–235211
Contact K M V Hall
Aims to promote communication between people and organisations actively involved in educational and vocational guidance. Membership mainly professional.
B V P

Micros and Primary Education
see p.14

Montessori Safety AMI (UK)
see p.6

National Association of Development Education Centres
6 Endsleigh Street, London WC1H 0DX
01–388 2670
Umbrella organisation which aims to promote the work of local development education centres, and to generate interest in the subject of development education. Can provide information about development education initiatives and projects in your area.
C B V P

National Association for Environmental Education
West Midlands College of Higher Education, Gorway, Walsall, WS1 3BD
0922–31200
Contact Philip Neal
An umbrella body which promotes an awareness of the need for environmental education. May be able to advise on local environmental education initiatives near you.
C B V P

National Association for Outdoor Education
50 High View Avenue, Grays, Essex RM17 6RU
Promotes the acceptance of appropriate outdoor education as an integral part of the UK education system. Provides information about opportunities for outdoor education.
B V P

National Centre for Play
Moray House College of Education, Holyrood Road, Edinburgh EH8 8AQ
031–556 8455 ext 329
Contact Elaine Drysdale/Nancy Ovens
Runs an information bank with over 3,000 items of play-related information, including equipment, special needs, child care and safety.

Anyone is welcome to visit the centre and refer to its resources. Training in play-related topics can also be provided on request.
C P

National Union of Students
461 Holloway Road, London N7 6LJ
01–272 8900
Contact Tim Walker
Can offer advice on student grants, student social security payments, and access to education.

Steiner Schools Fellowship
Kidbrooke Park, Forest Row, East Sussex RH18 5JB
0342–822115
Contact Peter Ramm
Can provide lists of Steiner schools and information about Steiner education. Helps parents to find the right Steiner school for their children. Promotes Steiner education through literature, talks and exhibitions.
C B P

Tavistock Institute of Medical Psychology
see under HEALTH, p.73

West-Central (Consultancy, Training and Community Research)
3 Gower Street, London WC1E 6HA
01–636 9766
Contact Steve Miller
A professional training and consultancy association for social and youth workers; publishes literature on topics such as 'Children and Family Break-Up in Anglo-Jewry'.
C P

World-Wide Education Service of the PNEU
Strode House, 44-50 Osnaburgh Street, London NW1 3NN
01–387 9228
Contact Benny Dembitzer

Helps parents (often English-speaking expatriates) to educate their children at home, and fosters the educational ideas and methods of Charlotte Mason. Provides a core-curriculum, educational equipment and books.
C P

CAMPAIGNING ORGANISATIONS AND PRESSURE GROUPS

Campaign for the Advancement of State Education
The Grove, High Street, Sawston, Cambridge CB2 4HJ
Contact Sue Hodgson
Aims for quality, equality and partnership between parents and teachers in state education. Maintains network of local groups.
B V P

Centre for Alternative Technology
Llwyngwern Quarry, Machynlleth, Powys, Wales SY20 9AZ
0654–2400
Contact Rick Dance
Maintains a permanent demonstration centre for alternative technologies (open to the public all year round); provides information; runs educational courses (some suitable for schools).
C V P

Centre for Studies on Integration in Education
4th Floor, 415 Edgware Road, London NW2 6NB
01–452 8642
Contact Mark Vaughan
Works to end segregation in education. Calls on local education authorities to provide appropriate support in mainstream schools for all children with disabilities or those who experience difficulties in learning.

Gives information and advice to parents and has a wide range of publications.
C P

Findhorn Foundation
The Park, Forres, Highland Region, Scotland IV36 0TZ
0309–30311
Contact Karin Aubrey
A community which runs a variety of educational programmes and courses for people concerned with encouraging spiritual and religious values in society. Visitors' programme available.
C B V P

Glosa Education Organisation
PO Box 18, Richmond, Surrey TW9 2AU
Contact Wendy Ashby
Encourages the teaching of the international language, Glosa, to all age groups.
C B V P

Minority Ethnic Teachers Association
8 Carmichael Place, Langside, Glasgow G42 9UE
041–649 0059
Contact Hakim Din
Campaigning organisation dedicated to promoting antiracism and racial equality in the field of education. Provides advice and support to people with similar objectives. Develops multicultural and antiracist guidelines on various aspects such as policies and currriculum initiatives.
V

Montessori Society AMI (UK)
26 Lyndhurst Gardens, London NW3 5NW
01–435 7874
Contact Secretary
Aims to help further understanding about the Montessori approach to

children. Publishes a booklist and a list of registered Montessori schools. Provides information for people interested in training to become a Montessori teacher. Holds open meetings, conferences and talks. Membership open to all.
V P

National Anti-Racist Movement in Education
PO Box 9, Walsall, West Midlands, WS1 3SF
0922–720824 ext 300
Contact S Shukla
Campaigns to bring about changes within the educational system that will lead to the development of a truly multiracial society.
B V P

National Association for the Support of Small Schools
91 King Street, Norwich, Norfolk NR1 1PH
0603–613008
Contact Molly Stiles
Provides a voice for and a link between all those who believe that small schools, particularly in rural areas, have educational and social roles too precious to loose. Offers advice and information to communities facing the loss of their local school.
B V P

National Childcare Campaign Ltd/ Daycare Trust
see under FAMILY WELFARE, p.29

National Committee on Racism in Children's Books
5 Cornwall Crescent, Basement Office, London W11 1PH
01–221 1353
Contact General Secretary
Campaigns against racism in children's books and in educational structures; promotes anti-racist

perspectives and initiatives. Produces quarterly magazine.
C P

National Convention of Black Teachers

PO Box 30, Pinner, Middx HA5 5EU
01–866 1682
Contact Raj Ray
Campaigns to fight discrimination and racism in all its manifestations in the field of education; to consider education in Britain from the point of view of the Black community; to provide a forum for co-operation between Black teachers and other interested individuals to work towards a fair and genuine system of multicultural education.
B V P

Network 81

52 Magnaville Road, Bishop's Stortford, Herts CM23 4DW
0279–503244
Contact Liz Arrondell/Rosie Johnson
0565–2666
Offers information, help and guidance on the workings of the 1981 Education Act, and supports parents of children with special educational needs. Campaigns to promote equality of opportunity in education for all children, and to further the concept of parent/professional partnership.
V B P

Royal Society for the Prevention of Cruelty to Animals

The Causeway, Horsham, Sussex RH12 1HG
0403–64181
Works to promote kindness and prevent cruelty to animals; runs an education programme in schools and colleges; has junior membership scheme.
C B P

Simplified Spelling Society

61 Valentine Road, Birmingham B14 7AJ
021–444 2837
Contact Christopher Upward
Aims to develop ways of modernising English spelling, to educate public opinion as to the need for and advantages of simplified spelling and to campaign for children to be taught simplified spelling.
V P

Social Morality Council

see under FAMILY WELFARE, p.27

Society for the Promotion of Vocational Training and Education (Skill-UK)

2 Beverley Gardens, Westbury on Trym, Bristol BS9 3PR
0272–683604
Contact W W Norris
Aims to raise the standards, skill and technical knowledge of young people. Organises teams of young craftsmen and women to compete in the International Youth Skill Olympics.
C P

Tidy Britain Group

The Pier, Wigan, WN3 4E
0942–824260
Contact Information Officer
Works for the prevention and control of litter; produces teaching materials and factsheets for schools and youth groups.
C B V

CHILDREN WITH PARTICULAR NEEDS

Advisory Council for the Education of Romany and other Travellers

Mary Ward Centre, 42 Queen Square, London WC1N 3AJ
01–831 7079

Contact Mary Waterson
Works with Travellers to promote consultation and co-operation with local and national authorities and to secure the provision of safe accommodation and all other community services, primarily education, for Gypsy Travellers.
C P

Afro-Caribbean Educational Resource Centre

Wyvil School, Wyvil Road, London SW28 2TJ
01–627 2662
Contact Librarian
Publishes materials for use in schools; runs young Black writers essay competition; maintains a reference library on all subjects related to the Black experience.
C P

Anthroposophical Society in Great Britain

Rudolf Steiner House, 35 Park Road, London NW1 6XT
01–723 4400
Contact Nick Thomas
Gives information on educational establishments, and on homes and farms for handicapped people; encourages all kinds of artistic activity and research.
C B V P

Association For All Speech-Impaired Children (AFASIC)

347 Central Markets, Smithfield, London EC1A 9NH
01–236 3632/6487
Contact Beatrice Sayers
Provides an information and advice service for professionals, young people and parents of speech-and-language-disordered children; encourages early assessment and diagnosis of these conditions; sponsors research; organises activity weeks; raises funds.
C B V P

Association of Educational Psychologists

3 Sunderland Road, Durham DH1 2LH
091–384 9512
Contact S W Cosser
The work of educational psychologists includes the assessment of children's educational needs, and the provision of strategies to meet those needs. Educational psychologists are committed to working closely with parents in these matters, in accordance with their code of professional conduct.
B P

Association of Workers for Maladjusted Children

Redhill School, East Sutton, Maidstone, Kent ME17 3DQ
0622–843104
Contact A J Rimmer
Multi-disciplinary association for all workers involved in provision for children with emotional and behavioural difficulties.
C B V P

British Dyslexia Association

98 London Road, Reading, Berks RG1 5AU
0734–668271/2
A federation of local dyslexia associations throughout the UK; aims to encourage better assessment and educational facilities for people with dyslexia.
C B V P

British Organisation for Rehabilitation Through Training

Whitehall Court, London SW1 2EL
01–839 4045
Runs a number of training and educational schemes for young people in need; part of a world-wide organisation.
C B V P

Dyslexia Institute
133 Gresham Road, Staines, Middx
TW18 2AJ
0784–63851
Gives advice to parents and teachers
and provides expert assessment of
learning difficulties, and appropriate
tuition.
C P B V

Friends for the Young Deaf Trust
see under HANDICAP, p.59

Gifted Children's Information Centre
Hampton Grange, 21 Hampton Lane,
Solihull B91 2QJ
Contact Dr Peter Congdon
Offers information, advice and
counselling to parents of gifted
children. Arranges psychological
assessments for gifted children, and
for those with dyslexia and handicaps.

Joint Educational Trust
38 Hillsborough Road, London
SE22 8QE
Contact Virginia Pim
Gives children an opportunity to offset
emotional pressures, disability, and
other problems in a different
environment. Priority given to children
of primary school age.
C V

KIDS
80 Waynflete Square, London
W10 6UD
01–969 2817
Runs a portage association which
provides weekly home visits by
trained visitors who show parents
how to introduce direct teaching
techniques into the daily care of their
child with developmental or learning
problems. Provides counselling, visits
and outings, parents' meetings and a
toy library.
C B V

National Association for Gifted Children
1 South Audley Street, London
W1Y 5DQ
01–499 1188
Promotes the welfare of gifted
children, their parents and their
families; disseminates information
concerning gifted children.
C B V P

National Association for Remedial Education
2 Lichfield Road, Stafford ST17 4JK
0785–46872
Contact C Gallow
Provides a service to teachers helping
pupils who have learning problems;
publishes practical guides for
teachers, some of which are designed
for use in schemes where staff and
parents work together.
C B V P

National Gypsy Council (Romani Kris)
Greengate Street, Oldham, Greater
Manchester OL4 1DG
061–665 1924
Contact Hughie Smith
Works with education authorities to
obtain a good education for Gypsy
children within the framework of an
integrated state school system.
C B V P

National Gypsy Education Council
22 Northend, Warley, Brentwood,
Essex CM14 5LA
0272–219451
Contact Thomas Acton
Offers assistance to parents in dealing
with local education authorities; runs
an information and publications
service; holds meetings.
C B V P

National Library for the Handicapped Child

Institute of Education, 20 Bedford Way, London WC1M 0AL
01–636 1500
Contact Juli: Braithwaite/ Beverley Mathias
Provides a reference and information service concerning children whose handicap affects their ability to read. Children's books and non-book materials are on display, plus reference books and journals. Visitors welcome, but please contact the library beforehand.
C P

National Network of Deaf Students

see under HANDICAP, p.60

Parents in Partnership

25 Woodnook Road, London SW16 6TZ
01–677 9828
Contact Margaret Gault
Works to advance the educational facilities offered to children with special needs (as defined in the Education Act 1981). Offers support and advice to parents, organises local parent groups.
B

Pestalozzi Children's Village Trust

Sedlescombe, Battle, Sussex TN33 0RR
042487–444
Contact Alan Hatter
Maintains a 'village' where children in need may live and be educated in groups in the traditions of their own country of origin; after schooling, the children return to their home countries. Runs a sponsorship scheme for 'parents' to support individual children.
C B V P

Potential Trust and Questors

7 Bateman Street, Headington, Oxford, Oxon OX3 7BG
0865–750360
Contact Anna Comino-Janes
Helps children with special needs arising from a high degree of unfulfilled potential by providing activities to complement the normal range of work and recreation encountered at home and school. Involved in the provision of residential activities for children/parents, prepares educational materials, and provides information for families.
C V

Rathbone Society

1st Floor, Princess House, 105/107 Princess Street, Manchester M1 6DD
061–236 5358
Organises supportive community and social work on behalf of children and young people with learning difficulties and their families. Runs parent support groups, befriending schemes, pre-school playgroups, community education activities, clubs for school children, literacy schemes, drop-in centres etc, throughout the country. Publishes guidelines for parents on 1981 Education Act – Children with Special Educational Needs.
C B V P

Service Away from Home

247 Pentonville Road, London N1 9NJ
01–278 2071
Contact Sylvia Nair
Runs a youth training scheme for young people who will benefit from undertaking their training away from home in community care.
C

Skill – National Bureau for Students with Disabilities

see under HANDICAP, p.53

Toy Aids
Lodbourne Farm House, Lodbourne Green, Gillingham, Dorset SP8 4EA
07476–2256
Contact Don Packwood
Provides toys and educational aids for use by disabled children.

Volunteer Reading Help
Ebury Teachers' Centre, Sutherland Street, London SW1V 4LH
01–834 6918
Contact Caroline Dale
Provides help and encouragement for children aged 7-ll who lack confidence and skill in their reading; trains volunteers to help with these under-achievers.
C B V

PARENTHOOD

Exploring Parenthood
Omnibus Workshop, 41 North Road, London N7 9DP
01–607 9647
Runs day workshops in London for parents where common problems of parenting can be discussed with professionals from the field of child and family development. Runs workshops for parent groups in schools or organisations in London and throughout the country. Trains parents who would like to run parent support groups in their own community.
C V P

Pagan Parenting Network
Blaenberem, Mynyddcerrig, Llanelli, Dyfed SA15 5BL
Offers support to parents who wish to bring up their children in harmony with Mother Earth, and in accordance with traditional spirituality.
P

Parent Network
see under FAMILY WELFARE, p.38

PARTICULAR SUBJECTS

Afro-Caribbean Resource Centre Ltd
339 Dudley Road, Winson Green, Birmingham B18 4HB
021–455 6382
Provides training workshops and education in communications skills for young unemployed people and others; promotes business development, co-operative ventures; runs a library and information service. Encourages the sharing of experience, contacts and resources.
B V

AIDS Care, Education and Training (ACET)
see under HEALTH, p.73

Archaeology in Education
Department of Prehistory and Archaeology, University of Sheffield, Sheffield, S10 2TN
0742–768555 ext 6081
Contact Professor Keith Branigan
Gives information and advice on careers in archaeology and courses at university; provides general and up-to-date information on archaeology; produces audio-visual aids on prehistory and archaeology.
V P

Association for Science Education
College Lane, Hatfield, Herts AL10 9AA
0707–267411
Promotes and encourages science education in schools and colleges. The majority of its members are practising teachers. Also provides a means of communication for all concerned with the teaching of

science in schools and with education in general.
C B V P

Breakout Theatre Company
Interchange, 15 Wilkin Street, London NW5 3NG
01–485 2848
Contact Suzanne Rider
A theatre-in-education company, concerned to explore issues of oppression through performance and workshops.
P

British Association for the Advancement of Science
Fortress House, 23 Savile Row, London W1X 1AB
01–494 3326
Runs a programme of national and local events, designed to interest children and young people in science and technology. Has separate youth section, BAYS, which organises competitions and a science fun day.
C B V P

Centre for World Development Education
Regent's College, Regent's Park, London NW1 4NS
01–487 7410
Can provide information and educational materials for local groups, parents, teachers and churches about world development issues, and about Britain's interdependence with developing countries.
C V P

Choir Schools Association
c/o Hon Secretary, Westminster Cathedral Choir School, Ambroseden Avenue, London SW1P 1QH
01–834 9247
Contact Peter Hannigan
Provides parents with information and literature about choir schools.
B P

Christian Education Movement
PO Box 36, Isleworth, Middx TW7 5DU
01–847 0951
Contact Brenda Lealman/Stephen Orchard
Can provide information about religious education, and supply leaflets and other publications on religious education in schools.
C B V P

Civic Trust Education Group
17 Carlton House Terrace, London SW1Y 5AW
01–530 0914
Contact Celia Clark
Works with schools, local planning authorities and environmental groups to demonstrate ways in which the knowledge and experience of planners, architects and other professionals can be used to help with the teaching of environmental studies (especially concerning the built environment) in schools.
C B V P

Commonwork Land Trust
Bore Place, Chiddingstone, Edenbridge, Kent TN8 7AR
0732–463225
Contact Margaret Williams
Develops educational projects on ecology, arts, health, development education for use with schools and with handicapped people. Produces educational materials for sale.
C V P

Council for Education in World Citizenship
19–21 Tudor Street, London EC4Y 0DJ
01–353 3353
Aims to promote international understanding; organises conferences for 13/14 year olds and 14/18 year olds; provides information;

distributes UN literature; publishes resource guides.
C B V P

Council for Environmental Education

School of Education, University of Reading, London Road, Reading RG1 5AQ
Co-ordinating body for a large number of national and local organisations concerned with environmental education. Maintains resource centre of educational materials; runs information service.
C P

Council on International Educational Exchange

Seymour Mews House, Seymour Mews, London W1H 9PE
01–935 5594
Contact Dr Michael Woolf
A private, non-profit-making organisation which works to develop, serve and support international education as a means of building understanding and peaceful co-operation among nations.
C B P

Faculty of Church Music

see under LEISURE, p.95

Festival of Languages and Young Linguists Awards

Marton, Rugby CV23 9RY
0926–632335
Contact Christine Wilding
Organises biennial national festival and a variety of regional and local events to promote language learning.
C B V

GAMMA (Gender and Mathematics Association)

Faculty of Education, Goldsmith's College, University of London, New Cross, London SE14 6NW
01–692 7171

Contact Lesley Jones
Aims to study and encourage mathematical education for girls; produces newsletters; holds conferences, including 'Maths and Your Future', for 6th form girls.
B V P

Islamic Foundation

223 London Road, Leicester LE2 1ZE
0533–700725
Contact S F Ahmad
A Muslim research and publication organisation; produces books and other teaching materials on Islam for parents and children; gives advice on religious matters.
C V P

Jewish Education Bureau

8 Westcombe Avenue, Leeds LS8 2BS
0532–663613
Contact Rabbi Douglas S Charing
Promotes the study of Judaism as a world religion in British schools and colleges; produces a catalogue of publications suitable for use at GCSE and A Level (SAE, please). Can answer enquiries on religious and multicultural education from parents and teachers.
B V P

JMB Development Training

1 Thorpe Close, London W10 5XL
01–960 5847/01–969 7752
Contact Margo Gulvin
Runs short personal development courses for young people, including school-leavers, unemployed young people, and young people at work. Courses may be requested by employers, teachers, voluntary youth organisations, etc.
C V

Marine Society

202 Lambeth Road, London SE1 7JW
01–261 9535

Contact Richard M Frampton
Aims to encourage young people to
make a career at sea; establishes
links between schools and ships;
gives grants to maritime youth
organisations; provides scholarships
for young seafarers; runs sea training
ships.
C V P

Micros and Primary Education

7 Holme Drive, Sudbrooke, Lincoln
LN2 2SF
0522–754408
Contact G E Jones
Promotes the use of microcomputers
in primary education; produces a
journal and special reports, also
program disks. Holds annual
conference and regional day schools.
C B V P

Minaret House

9 Leslie Park Road, Croydon, Surrey
CRO 6TN
01–654 8801/01–681 2972
Contact R El Droubie
Publishes materials for religious
education in schools; will try to
provide information to enquirers on a
voluntary basis.
C P

Modern Languages Association

Regent's College, Inner Circle,
Regent's Park, London NW1 4NS
01–487 7439
Contact Elizabeth Ingham
Offers information concerning the
study of languages at any level and for
any purpose. Publishes various guides
designed to help pupils and their
parents.
C B V P

Mudiad Ysgolion Meithrin

10 Park Grove, Cardiff, Wales
0222–236205
Contact J B Jones
Gives advice and information about
Welsh-medium education (including
pre-school); offers advice and support
regarding integration to parents of
pre-school children with special
needs; offers guidance to parents on
their educational role; advises
English-speaking parents on how to
help their children become bilingual.
C B V P

National Christian Education Council

Robert Denholm House, Nuffield,
Redhill, Surrey RH1 4HW
Contact Eric Thorn
Produces publications about Christian
education, and books for children.
C B V P

National Council for Schools' Sports

35 Holywell Close, Farnborough,
Hants GU14 8TS
0252–519312
Contact Mike Stringer
Co-ordinates the work of schools'
national sports associations (currently
covering 22 different sports),
represents their views, provides a
forum for discussion, and
disseminates information.
C V P

National Resource Centre for Dance

University of Surrey, Guildford, Surrey
GU2 5XH
0483–509316
Contact Judith Chapman/Kate King
Aims to make visual, written and
sound resources for dance easily
available; works to establish a dance
archive; publishes books and other
information materials, some suitable
for GCSE; answers enquiries;
provides information.
C V P

Operation Raleigh (The Scientific Society Ltd)

see under LEISURE, p.93

School Natural Science Society

153 Fernside Avenue, Hanworth,
Middx TW13 7BX
Contact Diane S Jackson
Concerned with science and
technology education in primary
schools. Can offer advice and
information.
C P

Sing for Pleasure Trust

25 Fryerning Lane, Ingatestone,
Essex CM4 0DD
Contact Lynda Parker
Promotes music education; runs a
wide variety of courses, including
ones for children, teachers and
schools.
C B V P

Society for Education through Art

Bath Academy of Art, Corsham,
Wiltshire SN13 0DB
0249–712571
Contact Derek Pope
Aims to encourage all opportunities
for creative work within the
educational system; provides
information and advice for teachers
and concerned parents.
C B V P

Society for Education in Film and Television

29 Old Compton Street, London
W1V 5PL
01–734 3211/5455
Contact Sean Cubitt
Promotes education about all aspects
of the media; provides advice,
training, publications and teaching
materials for all ages.
C B V P

Society for Italic Handwriting

Highfields, Nightingale Road,
Guildford, Surrey GU1 1ER
Contact John Fricker
Seeks to promote the everyday use of
italic handwriting as an elegant and
legible script.
C V P

Standing Conference on Schools' Science and Technology

1 Birdcage Walk, London SW1H 9JJ
01–222 7899
Contact Information Officer
Promotes the development of science
and technology in schools; runs
science clubs (Young Engineers Club)
and an award scheme (CREST) for
young people; fosters links between
schools and industry.
C B V P

Student Christian Movement

186 St Paul's Road, Balsall Heath,
Birmingham B12 8LZ
021–440 3000
Contact Tim McClure
Encourages the study of the Christian
faith and a commitment to living the
Christian life.
C B P

Trident Trust

Robert Hyde House, 48 Bryanston
Square, London W1H 7LN
01–723 3281
Contact Bob Newman
Encourages links between 4th and 5th
year secondary school pupils and
industry; arranges work experience
and community involvement
programmes.
C B V P

Union of Muslim Organisations of the UK and Eire

see under FAMILY WELFARE, p.22

United Kingdom Council for Music Education and Training

13 Back Lane, South Luffenham,
Oakham, Leics LE15 8NQ
0780–721115
Contact Linda Cummins

Can offer advice on music education and training in the UK.
C P

United Kingdom Initial Teaching Alphabet Association

181 Fleetwood Avenue, Holland-on-Sea, Essex CO15 5RA
0255–813768
Contact Ronald A Threadgall
Offers information and advice on the Initial Teaching Alphabet (ita); reading scheme, books, literacy programmes and parents' pack available.
C V P

United Kingdom Reading Association

c/o Edge Hill College of Higher Education, St Helen's Road, Ormskirk L39 4QP
0695–77505
Contact Hazel Clarke
Devoted to reading, language, communication and learning. Runs an information and advisory service for parents and teachers; organises family reading groups; publishes a journal, newsletter, books and pamphlets.
C B V P

Vivekananda Centre

c/o 41 Morris Avenue, Coventry CV2 5GU
0203–445044
Contact Information Officer

Arranges various educational and recreational events relating to ancient Indian art and culture; may be able to provide information about voluntary services for the Indian community.
V P

Wadada Educational Magazine

c/o Flat 6, 147 Coningham Road, London W12 8BU
01–740 7115/749 3252
Contact Rashida Ashanti
Publishes educational materials (some for children) designed to promote an understanding of the Rastafarian faith. Runs a women's group and a Saturday supplementary school for children aged 5–11.
B V

Watch Trust for Environmental Education

see under LEISURE, p.100

Young Enterprise

Ewert Place, Summertown, Oxford OX2 7B2
0865–311180
An organisation to promote commercial and industrial association. Gives young people between 15 and 19 the opportunity to set up and run model companies, using their own initiative, in an atmosphere of commercial realism.
C B V

FAMILY WELFARE

GENERAL ORGANISATIONS

RELATIVES OF PEOPLE WITH PROBLEMS

Al-Anon Family Groups UK and Eire
61 Great Dover Street, London
SE1 4YF
01–403 0888 (24-hour)
Contact Secretary
Runs two organisations, Al-Anon, to help families of alcoholics, and Alateen, to help teenagers (12–20) who are, or have been, affected by an alcoholic relative. Both offer help and support.
B V P

Catholic Social Service for Prisoners
189a Old Brompton Road, London
SW5 0AR
01–370 6612/0883
Assists prisoners and ex-prisoners (of any religion); gives support to their families and children.
C B V

Cultists Anonymous
BM Box 1407, London WC1N 3XX
Contact Mandy
Helps parents and other family members of people who have joined cults (new religious movements); assists cult members who have expressed an interest in receiving counselling. Runs 24-hour helpline; provides information about cults.
C V P

Drugline
9a Brockley Cross, London SE4 2AB
Contact Tim Green
Runs telephone advice/counselling service for drug users and their families; supports addicts, friends and relatives; maintains self-help groups.
C B V P

Eating Disorders Association
see under HEALTH, p.78

Families Anonymous
310 Finchley Road, London NW3 7AG
01–731 8060
Helps families and friends of drug abusers; aims to relieve distress and assist recovery. Runs self-help groups and a telephone helpline. All activities strictly confidential and anonymous.
B V P

Family Action Information and Rescue
BCN Box 3535, PO Box 12, London
WC1N 3XX
01–539 3940
Contact Ursula McKenzie
Counsels and assists people involved with extremist religious cults, their families and friends. Provides information about cults and their characteristics.
P

Gamblers Anonymous and Gam-Anon
17–23 Blantyre Street, Cheyne Walk, London SW10 0DT
01–352 3060
A self-help group of men and women who have joined together to do something about their own gambling problems. Gam-Anon offers friendship, practical help, comfort and

understanding to parents and partners of compulsive gamblers.

Help and Advice Line for Offenders' Wives (HALOW)

5 Onslow Road, Southampton
SO2 0JD
Contact Fiona Gudge
Offers advice and practical support to any relatives of men in prison (all counsellors are prisoners' relatives); maintains a 24-hour crisis phone line.
C B V

Hungerford Drug Project (Turning Point)

26 Craven Street, London WC2 5NT
01–930 4688
Provides information, advice and confidential counselling (appointment or telephone) to people with drug-related problems, their families and friends.
C

National Campaign Against Solvent Abuse

The Enterprise Centre, 444 Brixton Road, London SW9 8JE
01–733 7330
Contact Allan Billington
Offers counselling and advice to people with a solvent abuse problem within their families. Runs an education programme in schools etc to warn young people of the dangers of solvent abuse.
C B V P

National Schizophrenia Fellowship

79 Victoria Road, Surbiton, Surrey
KT6 4NS
01–390 3651/3
Co-ordinates the activities of local support groups for patients and their families; runs an information and advisory service; raises funds.
C B V P

Parents of Young Gamblers

Memorial School, Mount Street, Taunton, Somerset TA1 3QB
0823–256936
Contact J Roberts
Offers advice and literature to help parents whose children are addicted to gambling.

Prisoners' Wives and Families Society

245 Caledonian Road, London
N1 0NG
01–278 3981
Contact Pauline Hoare
Assists prisoners' families and friends by offering free advice, information and counselling.
C V P

Prisoners' Wives Service

51 Borough High Street, London
SE1 1NB
01–403 4091
Contact Rose Keane/Louise Ryan
Gives advice, help and information to the families and friends of people in prison; runs self-help groups (Inner London only).
C V

Schizophrenia, a National Emergency

see under HEALTH, p.73

Schizophrenia Association of Great Britain

see under HEALTH, p.73

Victim Support – National Association

Cranmer House, 39 Brixton Road, London SW9 6DZ
01–735 9166
Contact Martin Wright
Co-ordinating body for a network of local victims' support schemes, all designed to meet the particular needs of victims of crime, and their families.

Gives advice and support to new schemes. Can tell parents about their nearest scheme.
C B V P

Why Helpless Youngsters
41 Tarbert Walk, London E1 0EE
01–790 1478
Contact Rev David Paton
Aims to discourage young people from carrying offensive weapons, to educate parents in their responsibilities and to ban the sale of offensive weapons and violent literature. Runs a support scheme for parents whose children have been attacked.
B V P

SPECIAL GROUPS

Bangladesh Association
5 Fordham Street, London E1 1HS
01–247 3733
Contact M-A Samad Khan
Undertakes social and welfare work for the Bangladeshi community.

Bangladesh Women's Association
91 Highbury Hill, London N5 1SX
01–359 5836
Contact H A Khan
Aims to look after the overall welfare of Bangladeshi women and their families in the UK, mainly through advising and counselling.
B V

Camden Chinese Community Centre
173 Arlington Road, London NW1 7EY
01–267 3019
Contact Administrator
Offers information and advice on welfare benefits, housing, education and child care to members of the Chinese community in Camden and elsewhere.
C V

Caribbean House and Westindian Concern Ltd
Caribbean House, Bridport Place, London N1 5DS
01–729 0986
Contact Jacqueline Benn
Runs family-centred counselling service; maintains an Afro-Caribbean Intermediate Treatment Unit for young offenders; organises educational programmes for young black people.
C V P

Central British Fund for World Jewish Relief
Drayton House, Gordon Street, London WC1H 0AN
01–387 3925
Can advise and assist Jewish refugees and their families in the UK who have fled from racial or religious persecution in any part of the world.

Central Council for Jewish Social Service
Stuart Young House, 221 Golders Green Road, London NW11 9DW
01–458 3282
Contact Daphne Band
Provides information (and publishes a directory) of the whole range of Jewish social services available in the UK.
C P

Chinese Advice and Information Centre
68 Shaftesbury Avenue, London WC2H 8HL
01–836 8291
Contact L Tang
Welfare organisation, caring for the needs of the Chinese community (mainly, but not exclusively, in London), including the special needs of women and children.
C B V P

Confederation of Indian Organisations (UK)

11 North Avenue, Harrow, Middx HA2 7AE
Co-ordinates and services all Indian cultural, social and political organisations in the UK that wish to integrate into the British way of life without losing their Indian identity. Can give information about local organisations concerned with family welfare, education and children's activities to Indian parents.
B V

Cypriot Advisory Service

26 Crowndale Road, London NW1 1TT
01–388 7971
Contact Rena Georgiou or Maroulla Eugeniou
Provides advice and support to the Cypriot community, primarily in London.
V

Federation of Spanish Associations in the UK

116 Ladbroke Grove, London W1 5NE
01–221 2007
Contact Antonio Gentino or Emilio Fuentes
Provides an information and advisory service; co-ordinates the activities of Spanish organisations within the UK; organises meetings for Spanish women and young people.
B V P

Greek Cypriot Brotherhood

4 Porchester Place, London W2 3TL
01–723 4001/01–402 8904
Contact Andreas Karaolis
Aims to look after the needs of the Greek Cypriot community in Britain; arranges social, cultural and educational activities.
B V

India Welfare Society

11 Middle Row, London W10 5AT
Offers help to members of the Indian community in the UK who are in need, hardship or distress. Runs a counselling service for family and other problems.
C B V P

Indian Workers Association

112a The Green, Southall, Middx UB2 4BQ
01–574 6019/7283
Provides for the welfare of immigrants in the UK, through advice on immigration, race relations, housing and education.
C B

International Family Service for Overseas Students

5th Floor, 20 Waterloo Street, Birmingham B2 5TB
021–643 9539
Contact Philippa Smith
Provides a welfare and counselling service for overseas students and members of their families.
C V P

Jewish Bereavement Counselling Service

see p.40

Kurdish Cultural Centre

13–15 Stockwell Road, London SW9 9AU
01–247 6251
Contact D Miran
Aims to assist and advise the Kurdish community on matters relating to education, health, immigration, legal issues, housing and social welfare.
V P

Latin American Women's Rights Service

Beauchamp Lodge, 2 Warwick Crescent, London W6 6NO
01–289 1601

Provides advice and information on a wide range of social, health and welfare issues to Latin American women and their children. Active mainly in the Greater London area.
V P

League of British Muslims
41 Cecil Road, Ilford, Essex
01–594 9080/01–592 3050
Contact Ashraf Raja
Organises social, cultural and educational programmes; runs multi-racial youth advisory service; gives advice on nationality and family problems.
V P

League of Jewish Women
Woburn House, Upper Woburn Place, London WC1H 0EP
01–387 7688
Contact Linda Herbert
Runs a voluntary welfare service to help anyone in need, regardless of age, race, colour or creed. Runs an educational and training programme, to foster mutual co-operation and service to the community.
C B

Migrant Services Unit
c/o LVSC, 68 Chalton Street, London NW1 1JR
01–388 0241
Contact Pauline Cahill
Works with migrants, and with some refugees and asylum seekers. Offers support and services to encourage migrant communities to develop their own community services, to benefit people of all ages.
C B P

National Council of Hindu Associations
41 Morris Avenue, Coventry CV2 5GU
0203–445044
Contact K N Kalia
Co-ordinates the activities of Hindu

associations in their social, cultural, educational and religious work. May be able to advise on contacting member organisations.
C V P

National Ethnic Minority Advisory Council
2nd and 3rd Floors, 13 Macclesfield Street, London W1V 7HL
01–349 8765
Aims to promote the advancement of ethnic minority communities in the UK. Provides advice and assistance to ethnic minority groups and individuals on immigration, housing, education, translation and interpretation, social services.
B V

National Federation of Cypriots in Great Britain
4 Porchester Terrace, London W2 3TL
01–723 4001/01–402 8904
Contact Andras Karaolis
Promotes the interests of the Cypriot community in Britain; maintains local branches; fosters social, cultural, recreational and educational links between members of the Cypriot community.
B V

Overseas Mauritians Aid Trust
14 Birkbeck Road, London SW19 8NZ
Contact Herve Isabelle
Promotes the welfare of people of Mauritian origin in the UK and in Mauritius, with particular reference to the relief of poverty, suffering, distress and sickness, and educational advancement.
C

Pakistan Welfare Association
181 Haydons Road, London SW19 8T8
01–542 6176
Looks after the general welfare of Pakistanis in the UK, and aims to

preserve and promote goodwill and fraternity among the Pakistani community. Arranges a wide range of educational and recreational activities for families and children.
C B V

Sangam Association of Asian Women
235–237 West Hendon Broadway, London NW9 7DH
01–202 4629
Contact Usha Bhatt
Runs classes in Hindi, Gujerati and dance for children. Offers advice to parents on matters relating to children's health and education.
C V

Sikh Cultural Society of Great Britain
88 Mollison Way, Edgware, Middx HA8 5QW
Contact Information Officer
Provides information about Sikh religion, history and culture; assists in the celebration of Sikh festivals. Non-political.
B V P

Sikh Divine Fellowship
132 Eastcote Avenue, Greenford, Middx UB6 0NR
01–903 7143
Contact Information Officer
Aims to promote spiritual and moral development through discourses, seminars and religious gatherings, and to foster racial harmony and inter-faith dialogue.
B

Standing Conference of West Indian Organisations in Great Britain
5 Westminster Bridge Road, London SE1 7XW
01–928 7861/2
Contact Information Officer
Provides information to the West

Indian community; runs legal, counselling and welfare services, including a youth service.
B V P

Tibet Society and Tibet Relief Fund of the UK
Olympia Bridge Quay, 70 Russell Road, London W14
01–603 7764
Contact Information Officer
Assists Tibetan refugees and their families in the UK, promotes understanding between cultures.
C V P

Turkish Cypriot Cultural Association
14 Graham Road, London E8 1BZ
01–249 7410
Contact Ahmet Ertugan
Works to benefit the Turkish Cypriot community, largely in London, through educational, welfare and recreational activities. Runs various activities for young people, and offers counselling and support to women and single parents.
C B V

UK Asian Women's Conference
7 Pembroke Road, Moor Park, Northwood HA6 2HP
09274–24297
Contact Sharmi Patel
Gives information and advice to Asian women in Britain; supports voluntary help to local organisations.
B V P

Union of Muslim Organisations of the UK and Eire
109 Campden Hill Road, London W8 7TL
01–221 6608/01–229 0538
Contact Dr Syed Aziz Pasha
Can provide a syllabus for Islamic education; produces textbooks on Islam; offers advice on religious observance in state schools and help

in selecting single-sex schools for girls; runs a marriage counselling service.
B V P

Union of Turkish Women in Britain
110 Clarence Road, London E5 8J
01–986 1358
Contact Gulen Iyigen or Eileen
Provides support, advice and information for Turkish-speaking women in Britain; runs a translation service, recreational, educational and cultural activities.

Union of Turkish Workers
84 Balls Pond Road, London N1 4AJ
01–923 1202/1579
Aims to organise and support the Turkish-speaking community in the UK; provides a comprehensive advice, translation and interpreting service; arranges educational, sporting, social and cultural activities; gives information on welfare rights.
B V P

Vietnamese Refugee Community in London
Community Hall, North Peckham Estate, Hordle Promenade East, London SE15 6JB
01–703 0036
Contact Cam Nx
Provides help for Vietnamese refugees in need and their families; co-ordinates the activities of various local refugee groups based in London; undertakes press and information work.
C V P

Wandsworth Asian Centre
59 Trinity Road, London SW17 7SD
01–871 7772/3/4
Contact M A Bhatti
Works to meet the social and welfare needs of the Asian community, primarily in south-west London; runs many child-care and educational,

advice and counselling schemes.
V

West Indian Women's Association
71 Pound Lane, Willesden, London NW10 2HU
01–451 4827
Contact Lloyd Dayes
Runs welfare, educational, cultural and recreational services for women, plus activities for young people (8-15) primarily, but not exclusively, in the London borough of Brent.
C B

SUPPORTING FAMILY LIFE AND THE COMMUNITY

Association of Carers
21–23 New Road, Chatham, Kent ME4 4JQ
0634–813981
Offers advice, information, support and opportunities for self-help to carers of disabled people and/or elderly people. Runs self-help groups nationwide.
B V P

Association of Interchurch Families
The Old Bakery, Danehill, Sussex RH17 7ET
Contact Chris Bard
Acts as a link between committed Christians married to partners of different church allegiances. Arranges national, regional and local meetings for mutual support and the exchange of ideas.
C B P

British Red Cross Society
9 Grosvenor Crescent, London SW1X 7EJ
01–235 5454
Provides training in community service skills, to help people who cannot help themselves. 100,000 volunteers in 11,000 local centres. Part of International Red Cross, a

worldwide non-political and non-sectarian movement. Runs a youth section.
C B V P

Catholic Marriage Advisory Council
Clitherow House, 1 Blythe Mews, Blythe Road, London W14 0NW
01–371 1341
Contact Stuart Ritchie
Offers education, to adults and children, for marriage and family life; marriage counselling and a medical advisory service. Counsellors throughout Britain.
C B V

CFW – Concern for Family and Womanhood
Springfield House, Chedworth, Cheltenham GL54 4AH
0285–72454
Offers free, confidential advice and counselling to parents and young people on problems affecting family or sexual relationships. Provides free advice and information leaflets on sexual, moral and Christian aspects of life. Can occasionally offer a retreat for over-stressed parents.
C B V P

Child Poverty Action Group
4th Floor, 1–5 Bath Street, London EC1V 9PY
01–253 3406
Campaigns to eradicate child and family poverty; provides information on issues related to poverty and social security, offers help to advice agencies on social security benefits.
C V P B

Church Action on Poverty
27 Blackfriars Road, Salford, Lancs M3 7AQ
061–832 525
Campaigns for the elimination of poverty and for individual human

fulfilment; its concerns include child benefit, housing policy, low pay. Membership open to individuals or organisations. Publishes factsheets on campaign issues.
V P

Church Army
Independents Road, London SE3 9LG
01–318 1226
A missionary and welfare organisation, which works throughout the UK to alleviate distress wherever it is found. Runs hostels and youth centres for young people; undertakes social work with families. Can be contacted through parish clergy.
C B V

Exploring Parenthood
see under EDUCATION, p.11

Family Holiday Association
Hertford Lodge, East End Road, Finchley, London N3 3QE
01–349 4044
Contact Fiona Hills
Provides holiday grants for underprivileged families; who must be referred by social work agencies, or similar.
C B

Family Policy Studies Centre
231 Baker Street, London NW1 6XE
01–486 8211
A research organisation, describing and analysing family trends, and the impact of government policies upon the family. Publishes the results of its research.
C P

Family Research Trust
Clitherow House, 1 Blythe Mews, Blythe Road, London W14 0NW
01–371 1341
Contact Stuart Ritchie
Promotes and funds research into all aspects of marriage – sociological,

psychological, medical and sexual – and encourages ways of healing and strengthening family life.
C V P

Family and Social Action

120b West Heath Road, London NW3 7TY
01–485 7485
A Christian organisation. Provides community services and support and help for families in need.
C B V P

Family Welfare Association

501–505 Kingsland Road, London E8 4AU
01–254 6251
Contact Gaynor Humphries
Assists families in distress, and relieves poverty. Runs social work centres, a charities information service, an education grant advisory service, and almshouses for elderly people.
C V P

Family and Youth Concern

Wicken, Milton Keynes MK19 6BU
0908–57234
Contact Valerie Riches
Aims to preserve stable family life; undertakes research into the effects of marital breakdown and public education programmes on family welfare and personal relationships.
B V P

Federation of Independent Advice Centres

13 Stockwell Road, London SW9 9AV
01–274 1839/1878
Contact Dorothy Newton
Co-ordinates the work of independent advice centres throughout the UK. Can put parents in touch with an advice centre near them. Publishes a countrywide directory of independent advice centres.
C B V P

Frontier Youth Trust

130 City Road, London EC1V 2NJ
01–782 0013
Offers support and resources to Christians who are working with church-based youth projects, LEA clubs, or with unattached young people experiencing problems such as unemployment, homelessness and drug or alcohol abuse.
C B V P

Holiday Care Service

2 Old Bank Chambers, Station Road, Horley, Surrey RH6 9HW
0293–774535
Contact Information Department
Gives free advice to anyone, who, because of disability or special needs or family circumstances, has difficulty in finding a suitable holiday. Introduces volunteers as carers/ companions to disabled people and others who need help on holiday.
C V P

Home-Start Consultancy

140 New Walk, Leicester LE1 7JL
0533–554988
Contact Margaret Harrison
The co-ordinating body for Home-Start schemes, which offer friendship, support and practical advice to families with children under 5. Can advise on how to set up a Home-Start scheme in your area.
C B V P

Institute of Family Therapy

43 New Cavendish Street, London W1M 7RG
01–935 1651
Contact Clinical Administrator
Offers a clinical service to families who are experiencing psychological, behavioural or relationship problems, including problems centred on children or adolescents. Problems are viewed in a family context, and

families are helped to find their own solutions.
C

Life Style Movement

Little Gidding, Huntingdon PE17 5JR
08323–383
Contact Margaret Smith
Aims to inform, encourage and support people who are seeking to live more responsibly, so as to achieve a just and more ecologically sustainable society for all members of the human family and for future generations. Publishes information booklets and other educational materials.
B V P

Methodist Church Division of Social Responsibility

1 Central Buildings, London
SW1H 9NH
01–222 8010
Aims to stimulate and express Christian concern in moral, social and international affairs including (among others) housing, health and medicine, family life, drugs, alcohol and gambling, mass media, racial justice issues, and community relations.
P

Mothers' Union

Mary Sumner House, 24 Tufton Street, London SW1P 3RB
01–222 5533
Contact Margaret Chapman
A society within the Anglican Church, concerned to strengthen and preserve marriage and Christian family life. Undertakes a range of welfare work with parents and children, provides holidays for families under stress and runs a 'Message Home' telephone service for runaways.
C B V

National Association of Volunteer Bureaux

St Peter's College, College Road, Saltley, Birmingham B8 3TE
021–327 0265
The national co-ordinating body for local volunteer schemes; produces a directory of local volunteer bureaux, provides an information service on all matters relating to volunteering.
C V P

National Childminding Association

8 Masons Hill, Bromley, Kent
BR2 9EY
01–464 6164
Contact Sue Owen
Encourages contact and communication between childminders, and the setting up of local groups involving childminders and parents. Provides help and advice to childminders.
C B V P

National Family Conciliation Council

34 Milton Road, Swindon, Wilts
SN1 5JA
0793–618486
Contact Jenny Bassett
Promotes the establishment of independent family conciliation services, and supports those services already in existence. Can provide information on family conciliation services in your area.
C B

National Federation of Self-Help Organisations

Central Information Office: 150 Townmead Road, London SW6 2RA
01–731 4438/9/01–731 8440
Contact Dr Vince Hines
Co-ordinates and supports the activities of a wide variety of self-help and community organisations, including youth work, education,

housing, health, co-operative ventures and the arts.
B V P

Quaker Social Responsibility and Education
Friends House, Euston Road, London NW1 2BJ
01–387 3601
Runs working groups to discuss and consider various social and educational concerns. Provides information about Friends schools. Organises short social projects for volunteers to provide a service and to promote international understanding.
C B P V

Salvation Army
101 Queen Victoria Street, London EC4P 4EP
01–236 5222
Contact Captain Charles King
Maintains a great many welfare and missionary projects, to help all sectors of society. Activities designed for parents and children include evangelistic centres, youth clubs, Sunday schools, children's homes and nurseries, nursing homes for unmarried mothers, street rescue homes, holiday centres and camps, also a missing persons bureau.
C B V P

Social Morality Council
23 Kensington Square, London W8 5HN
01–937 8547
Contact David Ingram
Aims to promote morality in all aspects of the life of the community. Encourages moral education, in co-operation with parents, teachers and employers.
C V

Society of St Vincent de Paul
24 George Street, London W1N 5RB
01–935 7625

Contact L F Collett
Provides a wide range of charitable services, including homes for boys and for women, and holiday camps for children.
C B V

Soldiers' Sailors' and Airmen's Families' Association
16–18 Old Queen Street, London SW1H 9HP
01–222 9221
Contact C Hogg
Provides a welfare and advisory service for the families of service and ex-service men and women.
C B V

Union of Catholic Mothers of England and Wales
12 Washington Avenue, High Beech Glade, St Leonards on Sea, East Sussex TN37 7TG
Contact Terri Coombs
Supports Catholic married women aiming to live according to the Catholic ideal of marriage, and to bring up their children as practising Catholics and public-spirited citizens. Promotes Catholic education; offers help to families in difficulty.
C B V P

Women's Royal Voluntary Service
234/244 Stockwell Road, London SW9 9SP
01–733 3388
Contact Information Officer
A national community service which undertakes a wide range of welfare projects, including work with young families, children's holidays, holiday playgroups, mother and baby clubs and work with prisoners and their families. Offices throughout England, Scotland and Wales.
B C V

Young Women's Christian Association of Great Britain

Clarendon House, 52 Cornmarket Street, Oxford OX1 3EJ
0865–726110
Runs hostels, social, welfare and educational programmes for young women and girls.
C V B

ORGANISATIONS FOR CHILDREN

GENERAL

Barnardo's

Tanners Lane, Barkingside, Essex IG6 1QG
01–550 8822
Contact Dr William Beaver
Provides care and treatment, both residential and non-residential, for children in need, irrespective of creed or colour, especially those who are physically or mentally handicapped or emotionally disturbed.
C B V P

Boys' and Girls' Welfare Society

Schools Hill, Cheadle, Cheshire SK8 1JE
061–428 5256
Contact Susan Lamonby
Provides residential care and education for deprived, disadvantaged, handicapped or emotionally disturbed young people. Participates in community-based care and education projects. Undertakes research, publishing and training for professions caring for children and young people.
C V B P

Catholic Women's League

2 Greycoat Place, London SW1P 1SB
01–222 2495
Contact Joan Crossman
Members work with other social services on various welfare schemes, including child welfare.
C B V

Child Accident Prevention Trust

28 Portland Place, London W1N 4DE
01–636 2545
Contact Rosemary Grydon
Provides information on child accident prevention to professionals and to the general public.

Children's Society see Church of England Children's Society

Christian Children's Fund of Great Britain

52 Bedford Row, London WC1R 4LR
01–831 7145
Contact Jill Davies
An organisation which aims to attract sponsors in this country to support educational health care and nutrition work among very poor children in developing countries. UK sponsors are linked to individual children overseas, and may correspond and visit.
C V P

Church of England Children's Society

Edward Rudolf House, Margery Street, London WC1X 0JL
01–837 4299
Contact Christine Goodair
Aims to offer a comprehensive child-care service to any child or any family in need, whether spiritually, physically or emotionally, irrespective of colour, race or creed. Runs a wide variety of welfare and educational projects for children and young people.
C B V P

Contact-a-Family

16 Strutton Ground, London, SW1P 2HP
01–222 2695; contact line 01–222 2211

Contact Information Officer
Brings together families of children
with special needs within the same
neighbourhood; encourages the
formation of local and national self-
help groups. Runs an information
service on behalf of numerous multi-
and rare handicap groups throughout
the UK. Works closely with the In
Touch Trust.
C B

Friends of the Children Society

9 Priory Close, South Woodford,
London E18 2QT
01–504 4644
Contact Derek Stockdale,
Works to help the poorest, most
needy and deprived children, mainly in
London, and to provide clothing, food,
outings, parties and holidays.
C B V

Mixifren Association

38 Cranwich Road, London N16 5JN
01–800 5969
Contact Oswald Noblemunn
Provides hostel and nursery facilities
for children in needy circumstances,
and arranges a series of recreational
and educational activities for young
people.
C

National Association for the Welfare of Children in Hospital

Argyle House, 29-31 Euston Road,
London NW1 2SD
01–833 2041
Contact Pauline Shelley
Supports sick children and their
families, and works to ensure that
health services are planned with their
needs in mind. Maintains a network of
local branches.
C B V P

National Association of Young People's Counselling and Advisory Services

17–23 Albion Street, Leicester
LE1 6GD
0533–558763
Contact Alison McKay
Co-ordinating body concerned to
promote and encourage the growth of
young people's advisory and
counselling services. Can supply
advice and information on existing
services.
B V

National Childcare Campaign Ltd/ Daycare Trust

Wesley House, 4 Wild Court, London
WC2B 5AU
01–405 5617
Advocates flexible, affordable daycare
and free nursery education for
children under 5. Promotes good
practice in nursery education; gives
advice and support to parents and
other campaigning groups. Produces
publications.
B V P

National Children's Bureau

8 Wakley Street, Islington, London
EC1V 7QE
01–278 9441
A national inter-disciplinary
association concerned with children's
needs in the family, school and
society. Undertakes research, makes
representations to other bodies,
publishes information and discussion
materials.
C B V P

National Children's Centre

The Brian Jackson Centre, New North
Parade, Huddersfield, West Yorks
HD1 5JP
Contact Jacqui Morris
Runs supportive schemes for parents
and for ethnic minority families;
maintains advice and information

services on child care and education. Current projects include work with under fives, adolescents and solvent abusers.
C V P

National Children's Home
85 Highbury Park, London N5 1UD
01–226 2033
A Christian voluntary child care organisation, with responsibility for over 7,000 children in various forms of care. Also provides supportive help for young people and for families through preventive work, intermediate treatment, fostering, adoption, housing, day care and family advice centres.
C B V P

National Council of Voluntary Child Care Organisations
8 Wakeley Street, London EC1V 7QE
Contact Raymond Clarke
A co-ordinating body of organisations concerned with voluntary child care. May be able to refer parents to a specialist organisation near them.
C B P

Ockenden Venture
Ockenden, Guildford Road, Woking, Surrey GU22 7UU
04862–72012/4
Contact Terry Horton
Receives, cares for, supports, educates and ultimately resettles displaced children, students and families.
C B V

OMEP (World Organisation for Early Childhood Education)
Thomas Coram Foundation, 40 Brunswick Square, London WC1N 1AZ
Contact Margaret Hewitt, Huntcliffe over Lane, Baslow, Bakewell, Derbyshire DE4 1RT, 0246–882207
Aims to promote the education,

health and welfare of children and families.
C P

Rainer Foundation
227/239 Tooley Street, London SE1 2JX
01–403 4434
Contact Angela Richardson
Helps young people who suffer disadvantage and discrimination in society, through work with individuals and in community and residential projects. Especially active in the areas of young homelessness, young offenders and the social problems faced by young women.
C V

Sailors' Children's Society
Newland, Hull, North Humberside HU6 7RJ
0482–42331/2
Contact E Brown
Provides residential care or hostel accommodation for sailors' children; supports one-parent families.
C V

Shaftesbury Homes and 'Arethusa'
3 Rectory Grove, Clapham, London SW4 0EG
01–720 8709
Runs homes and arranges recreational and study breaks for children, young people and single parents in need.
C B V

Shaftesbury Society
2a Amity Grove, Raynes Park, London SW20 9LJ
01–956 6634
Contact Rosemary Ward
Runs inner-city missions, special schools for physically-handicapped children, residential hostels, holiday centres; undertakes welfare work with children and parents in need.
C B V P

Thomas Coram Foundation for Children

40 Brunswick Square, London
WC1N 1AZ
Contact Colin Masters
Provides a wide range of services for children and young people, including day care, special needs adoption placement service, welfare work with homeless families in bed and breakfast accommodation, and with adolescents leaving the care of the local authorities.
C P

VOLCUF (Voluntary Organisations Liaison Council for Under Fives)

77 Holloway Road, London N7 8JZ
01–607 9573
Contact Jennifer Harding
A national organisation of groups working with children under five and their families. Provides information, encourages liaison between groups, organises a programme of events designed to support the work of its members, and acts as an advocate on behalf of the voluntary sector.
C P

ABUSED CHILDREN

ChildLine Charitable Trust

Addle Hill Entrance, Faraday Building, Queen Victoria Street, London EC4V 4BU
01–236 2380/ChildLine – call free **0800–1111**
Contact Sarah Jane Vernon
Runs free national helpline for children with any problems. Maintains team of counsellors and trained volunteers to refer children to appropriate helping agencies.
C V

Childwatch

25A Beverly Road, Hull HH15 2JJ
0430–423824/0482 25552
Contact Dianne Core/Barbara Heelas

Campaigns for better preventive action against family violence and child abuse, and for classes in parenting to be made part of the school curriculum. Provides information and educational materials.
B V P

Incest Survivors in Strength

see p.39

Lifeline – Help for Victims of Violence in the Home

PO Box 251, Marlborough, Wilts SN8 1EA
Offers help, support and advice to families experiencing violence within the home; runs a counselling service, encourages self-help groups.
C B V P

London Rape Crisis Centre

see p.37

National Society for the Prevention of Cruelty to Children

67 Saffron Hill, London EC1N 8RS
01–242 1626
Contact Keith Bradbrook
Works to prevent child abuse and neglect in all its forms; gives practical help to families at risk; campaigns to increase public awareness of the problem; initiates research and new methods of treatment. Maintains network of child protection teams to offer 24-hour response to children and families; runs playgroups, family care schemes and drop-in centres.
C P

Standing Committee on Sexually-Abused Children

2nd Floor, Crown House, London Road, Morden, Surrey SM4 5DX
01–545 3428/9
Contact Bernadette Manning
Provides an education and

consultation service about child abuse for anyone working with children.
C

CHILDREN WITH BEHAVIOURAL PROBLEMS

Apex Trust
Brixton Hill Place, London SW2 1HJ
01–671 7633
Contact Information Officer
Operates community-based employment resource centres and employment prospects workshops for ex-offenders and for young people at risk.
C B V P

Creative and Support Trust
34a(Basement), Stratford Villas, London NW1 9SG
01–485 0367
Contact Jennifer Hicks
Provides support and runs workshops (based in London) for women and girls who have experienced imprisonment or detention of various kinds, in prisons, psychiatric units, foster homes and similar institutions, and those on probation.
C V

Crisis Counselling for Alleged Shoplifters
c/o National Consumer Protection Council, London NW4 4NY
01–202 5787 (after 7pm **01–958 8859** answerphone)
Contact Regina Dollar
Gives counselling and advice to people accused of shoplifting offences; particularly concerned to help children accused of shoplifting.
V

Friendship Trust
Hardley House, Wootton, Woodstock, Oxon OX7 1EP
0993–812765
Contact Margie McGregor

Aims to put children and young adults with behavioural problems in touch with caring and supportive adults, who can encourage them to pursue creative and constructive activities outside the home or school.
C B V

Streetwise Youth
c/o Flat 3b, Langham Mansions, Earls Court Square, London SW5 9UP
01–373 8860
Contact Ken Fortune
Maintains an information, advice and support service for young people who have become prostitutes, and offers them an alternative way of life. Liaises with parents, police, probation workers and the courts.
C V

Teen Challenge UK
see under HEALTH, p.65

CHILDREN WITH PARTICULAR NEEDS

Children's Cancer Help Centre
see under HEALTH, p.67

Children's Country Holidays Fund
see under LEISURE, p.103

Christians in Care
PO Box 41, Bognor Regis, West Sussex PO21 3PU
Contact Michael Helliwell
Provides information, support and advice services to young people in care, and also aims to advance the Christian faith among young people between 12 and 25 who have been in care.
C V P

Community Links
81 High Street South, East Ham, London E6 4EJ
01–472 6652
Contact Mandy Wilson
Runs an independent social action

centre, with activities for children, teenagers, parents, pensioners and people with disabilities. Co-ordinates two national projects, the National Tower Blocks Network and Action Match. Publishes National Tower Blocks Directory.
C V P

Hyperactive Children's Support Group

71 Whyke Lane, Chichester, Sussex
0903–725182
Contact Sally Bunday
Gives help and support to hyperactive children and their families; suggests ideas to help overcome this handicap. Maintains network of local groups; supplies Diet Information Handbook and leaflets.
C B V P

Invalid Children's Aid Nationwide

see under HANDICAP, p.51

KIDIHOLS

Kidihols Office, Weymouth and Portland Borough Council, Westwey House, Westwey Road, Weymouth, Dorset
0305–761222 ext 439
Contact Peter Sparks
Provides facilities for voluntary organisations or social services departments to sponsor seaside holidays for unaccompanied children or single-parent families. Runs an information service about the availability of such holidays.

Kith and Kids

Chestnut Cottage, Stanstead Road, Hunsdon, Herts SG12 8PZ
0920–870741
Contact Carol Schaffer
A parents' self-help group actively involved in the integration of handicapped children and adults within the community. Runs a variety of social, recreational and educational activities for handicapped children and their families.
C B V

London Youth Advisory Centre

26 Prince of Wales Road, London NW5 3LG
01–267 4792
Offers information, counselling and therapy to young (12–25) people who are depressed, anxious, confused, in difficulties with their family or with other relationships, or unable to find work.
C

MacIntyre

see under HANDICAP, p.49

Malcolm Sargeant Cancer Fund for Children

see under HEALTH, p.81

National Association of Young People in Care

Second Floor, Maranar House, 28–30 Mosley Street, Newcastle upon Tyne NE1 1DF
091–261 2178
Contact Louise Webb
Aims to improve the conditions of young people in care and after-care, and to promote their views and opinions. Gives advice by letter and telephone; maintains local groups.
B

POD Charitable Trust

4 Steeles Mews North, London NW3 4RJ
01–586 0071
Contact K Einhorn
Aims to improve the quality of life of children and young people with special needs by providing free entertainment in hospitals.
C B V

Rathbone Society

see under EDUCATION, p.10

Ravenswood Foundation
see under HANDICAP, p.49

REACH – the Association for Children with Hand or Arm Deficiency
see under HANDICAP, p.60

Society of Action for Children in Tower Blocks
62 Chelsea Reach Tower, Blantyre Street, London SW10 0EG
01–352 5135
Contact Paul Carroll/Bernardine Lawrence
Aims to make tower-block tenants throughout the UK aware of their just entitlements.

SOS Children's Villages UK
32 Bridge Street, Cambridge CB2 1UJ
0223–65589
Provides loving family care and a secure future for homeless orphaned and abandoned children throughout the world. UK Association offers Child and Village sponsorship.
C B V P

STEPS – National Association for Families of Children with Congenital Abnormalities of the Lower Limbs
see under HANDICAP, p.61

Toy Aids
see under EDUCATION, p.11

Voice for the Child in Care
60 Carysfort Road, London N8 8RB
01–348 2588
Contact Gwen James
Provides a network for people concerned with children in care; can give independent assistance to children in care when needed.
C V P

RELIGIOUS OR ETHNIC MINORITIES

Caribbean House and Westindian Concern Ltd
see p.19

Catholic Association of Young Adults
41 Cromwell Road, London SW7 2DH
01–589 7550
Contact Sean Burke
An organisation of young Catholic people, concerned to explore their faith and witness to their beliefs.
C V

Catholic Children's Society
73 St Charles Square, London W10 6EJ
01–969 5305
Provides adoption services for Catholic infants and for children with special needs. Also provides a range of community services through Family Centres in many London boroughs.
C B

Catholic Child Welfare Council
1a Stert Street, Abingdon, Oxon OX14 3JF
0235–21812
Contact Rt Rev Mgr Michael Connelly
Can put parents or professionals in touch with local representatives of their Diocesan child welfare society.
C B

Catholic Youth Service
39 Fitzjohn's Avenue, London NW3 5JT
01–435 3596
Can put parents in touch with local youth groups for Catholic children and young people.
C B V

Children and Youth Aliyah Committee for Great Britain and Eire

4a New College Parade, Finchley Road, London NW3 5ET
01–586 9221
Contact Executive Director
Works for the rescue, rehabilitation and education of children in Israel.
C B V P

Community Roots Trust

4 Warple Way, Acton Vale, London W3 6RQ
01–740 1122
Contact Janet Ferguson
Co-ordinating body, providing support and advice to black community organisations, particularly Afro-Caribbean ones, throughout the UK. Undertakes community work with young people.
C B

Federation of Bangladeshi Youth Organisations

Montefiore Centre, Deal/Hanbury Street, London E1 5JB
01–247 8818
Contact Lloyd Gee
Co-ordinates local Bengali youth organisations; organises sporting, cultural and educational activities; works for social justice and equality for the Bengali community in Britain.
B V P

International Catholic Society for Girls

St Patrick's International Centre, 24 Great Chapel Street, London W1V 3AF
01–734 2156/01–439 0116
Contact Sister Sheelah Clarke
An international organisation which aims to look after young girls away from home. In the UK, is especially concerned to help au-pairs. Offers advice, information, counselling and a daily social programme of events.
C V

Jewish Blind Society (incorporating The Jewish Association for the Physically Handicapped)

see under HANDICAP, p.59

National Association of Asian Youth

46 High Street, Southall, Middx UB1 3DB
01–574 1325/5900
Contact Ravi Jain
An umbrella organisation to help young Asian people form groups and co-ordinate their activities. Provides specialist youth services. Represents the views of Asian youth at a national level. May be able to provide information about local Asian youth groups.
C B V P

Norwood Child Care

221 Golders Green Road, London NW11 9DL
01–458 3282
Contact Juliet Moss
Provides welfare services (including residential and foster care and welfare advice) to Jewish children who are handicapped, neglected, rejected or disadvantaged, and to their families.
C B V

ORGANISATIONS FOR PARENTS

ADOPTION AND FOSTERING

British Agencies for Adoption and Fostering

11 Southwark Street, London SE1 1RQ
01–407 8800
Contact Prue Chennells
Aims to promote good standards of practice in adoption, fostering and social work with children and families. Runs an advisory service for the public; organises an exchange

placement scheme for children with special needs.
P

Children First in Trans-Racial Fostering and Adoption

662 High Road, London N12 0NL
01–341 7190
Campaigning organisation (membership includes concerned adoptive parents) which aims to dissuade local authority and other agencies from practising bans on trans-racial adoptions and foster placements.

Independent Adoption Service

121 Camberwell Road, London SE5 0HB
01–703 1088
Contact Jane Dunbar
Aims to find permanent families, both foster and adoptive, for children of all ages; special emphasis is placed on working with black families and black children.
C P

Mission of Hope for Children's Aid and Adoption

14 South Hill Park Road, Croydon, Surrey CR2 7YB
01–688 0251
Provides Christian care for children and unmarried mothers; runs an approved adoption agency.
C

National Adoption Society

115 Park Street, London W1Y 4DY
01–624 3411
Contact D M Dye
A non-denominational society which tries to find the best possible home for each baby in its care. Runs welfare services for unmarried mothers.
C V

National Foster Care Association

Francis House, Francis Street, London SW1P 1DE
01–828 6266
Contact Pat Verity
Aims to improve the quality of the foster care service in the UK; supports self-help foster groups and associations; offers advice and information; runs training courses.
C B V P

National Organisation for Counselling Adoptees and their Parents

3 New High Street, Headington, Oxford OX3 5AJ
0865–750554
Contact Linda Savell
Runs a telephone listening, advice and counselling service. Gives assistance to adoptees searching for information about their origins and runs an intermediary service for adoptees and their birth relatives interested in making contact.
B V P

Parent to Parent Information on Adoption Services

Lower Boddington, Daventry, Northants NN11 6YB
0372–60295
Contact Philly Morrall
Helps potential adopters by passing on information about how and where to apply for children, especially children with special needs who would otherwise grow up in care. Offers support to members who have already adopted.
C B V P

Parents for Children

222 Camden High Street, London NW1 8DR
01–485 7526/7548
Acts as a voluntary adoption agency for school-age children and for children with disabilities.
C P

Post-Adoption Centre

Interchange Building, 15 Wilkin Street, London NW5 3NG
01–284 0555
Contact Phillida Sawbridge
Offers counselling, advice and support for adoptive families, adopted people and parents whose child has been adopted.
C P

World Family (Foster Parents Plan (UK))

315 Oxford Street, London W1R 1LA
01–493 0940/01–409 1667
Contact Stephanie Smith
Encourages people in the UK to take an interest in, and help to support, children and their families in the developing world, so as to improve the living conditions, educational opportunities and health care of these children and the communities in which they live.
C B V P

PARENTS AND GRANDPARENTS

British Organisation of Non-Parents

BM Box 5866, London WC1N 3XX
Contact Root Cartwright
Seeks to eliminate the cultural bias against non-parents in society and in the media by defending the choice to remain childfree and by emphasising the responsibilities involved in child-rearing. Parents and non-parents may join.
P

Catholic Needlework Guild

c/o 80 Wardle Chase, Walton on the Naze, Essex CO14 8QW
The Guild may be able to assist with knitted clothing for small children whose parents through unfortunate circumstances are unable to provide it themselves.
C B

Children Need Grandparents

2 Surrey Way, Laindon West, Basildon, Essex
0286–41607
Contact R C Fryer
Campaigns to change current legislation regarding rights of access by grandparents to children who are not in care; offers advice and assistance to grandparents who have been refused access to their grandchildren.

Families Need Fathers

BM Families, London WC1N 3XX
Contact Hon Secretary
Supports men and women with child custody problems following separation and divorce; promotes research into the problems faced by children from broken homes. Runs 'Walk-In-Talk-In' sessions at the Artists' Room, Conway Hall, Red Lion Square, London WC1 from 7.30 to 9.30 pm on the first and third Fridays of each month, and in other cities.
C B P

Kidscape

82 Brook Street, London,W1Y 1YG
01–493 9845
Contact Michele Elliott
Provides information and teaching materials for parents and other concerned adults to help them teach children practical and positive ways of dealing with potentially dangerous situations, including the possibility of sexual abuse.
P

London Rape Crisis Centre

PO Box 69, London WC1X 9NJ
01–837 1600 (counselling line);
01–287 3956 (office)
An organisation run by women to offer support and counselling to women and girls who have been raped or sexually assaulted.
C V P

Maternity Links
see under HEALTH, p.71

Meet-a-Mum Association
5 Westbury Gardens, Luton,
Bedfordshire LU2 7DW
0582–422253
To help mothers suffering from post-
natal depression, or who feel lonely
and isolated, through counselling,
practical one-to-one support and
group therapy; offering support and
advice to mothers of young children.
C B V

Mothers Apart from their Children
c/o BM Problems, London WC1N 3XX
Contact Ann John/Margaret Pearce
Offers help, support and
understanding to mothers separated
from their children; encourages the
formation of local support groups;
refers enquirers to other helpful
organisations if appropriate.
B V

Mothers' Union
see p.26

National Childminding Association
see p.26

Parent Network
44–46 Caversham Road, London
NW5 2DS
01–485 8535
Contact Cathie Black/Ginny Dodd
Aims to improve communications
between parents and children by
setting up a national network of
parent support groups; provides
support for parents and group leaders.
C B V P

Practical Alternatives for Mums, Dads and Under-Fives
c/o 162 Holland Road, Hurst Green,
Oxted, Surrey RH8 9QB
Contact Chrissie Denham
Promotes improved facilities for

parents who have children under five;
provides a directory of information
about these facilities for one locality;
may be able to advise on preparing
similar directories for your own
locality.
C V P

Twins and Multiple Births Association
41 Fortuna Way, Aylesby Park,
Grimsby, South Humberside
DN37 9SJ
0786–72080
Contact Jenny Smith
Gives encouragement and support to
parents of twins, triplets or more;
maintains a national register of twins
clubs. Has 200 branches countrywide.
Publishes leaflets on all aspects of
coping with multiples.
C B V P

We Welcome Small Children National Campaign
93a Belsize Lane, London NW3 5AY
01–586 3453
Contact Julie Jaspert
Works to promote the provision of
good facilities for parents or carers
with young children in public places,
shops, restaurants etc.
B V P

Women's Aid Federation, England
PO Box 39l, Bristol BS99 7WS
0272–420611 (information); 0272–
428368 (national helpline)
Provides information and temporary
refuge for women and their children
who are threatened by mental,
emotional or physical violence, or
sexual abuse. Maintains 120 locally-
based groups which provide
information, advice and refuge.
B V P

Working Mothers' Association
77 Holloway Road, London N7 8J2
01–700 5771

Contact Lucy Daniels
Provides information and advice about childcare provision to enable parents to make the best possible choice for their child. Maintains network of local groups; puts mothers in touch with other parents facing similar problems.
C B P

Workplace Nurseries Ltd
Room 205, Southbank House, Black Prince Road, London SE1 7SJ
01–582 7199/587 1456
Contact Penny Craig
Encourages the development of workplace nurseries to meet the needs of working parents and the social, educational and welfare needs of their children. Provides information and advice to parents and employers.
V P

PARENTS UNDER STRESS

Acceptance Helpline for Parents of Homosexuals
64 Holmside Avenue, Halfway Houses, Sheerness, Kent ME12 3EY
0795–661463
Contact Jill Green
Runs a telephone helpline (Tues - Fri 7.00 pm - 9.00 pm) for parents concerned about their son's or daughter's homosexuality. Organises a support group for parents; meetings currently based in Kent but expansion possible.
V P

Association of Crossroads Care Attendant Schemes Ltd
10 Regent Place, Rugby, Warks CV21 2PN
0788–73653
Maintains a network of local care schemes to relieve stress in families and others who care for disabled people. Works closely with existing statutory services.
C B P

Compassionate Friends
6 Denmark Street, Bristol BS1 5DQ
0272–292778
Contact Anne Pocock
Offers friendship and support to grieving parents who have lost a child through illness, accident, murder or suicide.
C B P

Cruse – Bereavement Care
Cruse House, 126 Sheen Road, Richmond,Surrey TW9 1UR
01–940 4818
Offers counselling, advice, and the opportunity for social contact to all bereaved people. Publishes a wide range of supportive literature.

CRY-SIS
BM CRY-SIS, London WC1N 3XX
01–404 5011
Contact Wendy Goodwin
Provides emotional support and practical advice to parents of babies who cry incessantly and have sleep problems; offers information about the possible causes of such behaviour. Maintains national network of self-help groups.
B V P

Foundation for the Study of Infant Deaths
see under HEALTH, p.70

Incest Survivors in Strength
c/o South London Women's Centre, 55 Acre Lane, Brixton, London SW2 5TN
01–326 1363/0333
Contact Jill Sullivan/Denise Rodricks
Aims to set up a national registry of incest survivor groups, for women only, offering support, encouragement and guidance.
Aims to increase public awareness of the long-term effects of the sexual abuse of children. Offers counselling, encouragement and guidance.

Produces literature.
C B V P

Jewish Bereavement Counselling Service

1 Cyprus Gardens, London N3 1SP
01–387 4300 ext 227/01–349 0839
(24 hour answerphone)
Contact June Epstein
Offers emotional help and support to members of the Jewish community who have been bereaved; acts as a resource and information centre on bereavement and Jewish beliefs and customs; maintains a network of trained counsellors.
V B P

Jewish Marriage Council

23 Ravenshurst Avenue, London NW4 4EL
01–203 6311
Contact Jeffrey Blumenfeld
Provides counselling for anyone under stress or with a problem concerning relationships, whether single, married or divorced; offers preventative counselling and advice in the form of group discussions to schools, youth clubs etc, and a wide range of other services.
C B V P

Life Care and Housing Trust

118–120 Warwick Street, Leamington Spa, Warks CV32 4QY
0926–21587/311667/316737
Contact Ann Dibb
Aims to relieve poverty, sickness and distress of pregnant women and unsupported mothers with one or more infant children by providing accommodation and making grants of equipment and money or clothing and offering counselling and advice.
C B V P

Lifeline – Help for Victims of Violence in the Home

see p.31

Miscarriage Association

18 Stonybrook Close, West Bretton, Wakefield, West Yorks WF4 4TP
0924–85515
Contact Kathryn Ladley
Provides information and support for women and their families both during and after miscarriage.
C B V P

National Council for the Divorced and Separated

13 High Street, Little Shelford, Cambridge CB2 5ES
021–588 5757
Contact Pat Partridge
Promotes the interests and welfare of all people whose marriages have ended in divorce or separation; arranges counselling, runs a postal advisory service, organises social events.
C B V P

Parent Line

Memorial School, Mount Street, Taunton, Somerset TA1 3QB
0823–256936
Contact Christine Ross
Offers help and advice to parents under stress.
V

Parentline-OPUS

106 Godstone Road, Whyteleafe, Surrey CR3 0GB
01–645 0469
Contact Carole Baisden
Aims to prevent child abuse and the maltreatment of infants and young children. Maintains a network of self-help groups for parents under stress; runs a befriending service, helplines and drop-in centres.
C B V P

Parents Against INjustice (PAIN)

Conifers, 2 Pledgdon Green, Nr Henham, Bishops Stortford, Herts CM22 6BN

0279–850545/850194
A self-help support group which aims to relieve the distress and suffering, and to protect the health, of parents who claim to have been wrongly accused of child abuse or neglect. Offers advice and support and liaises with solicitors and advises about professionals prepared to give second opinions.
B V P

Parents Aid

66 Chippingfield, Harlow, Essex
CM17 0DJ
0279–36597
Offers help, advice and practical support to families whose children are in social services care, or whose children are adopted without their consent. Publishes 'Guide for Families with Children in Care'.
B V P

Parents Anonymous

6–7 Manor Gardens, London N7 6LA
01–236 8918 (24-hour answering service)
Contact Sally Sturgeon
Offers friendship and help to parents who are tempted to abuse their child, or who have done so. Provides information, telephone counselling, visiting service for parents; arranges professional help and contacts for mutual support among parents.
B

Parents' Lifeline

Station House, 73d Stapleton Hall Road, London N4 3QF
01–263 2265/254 2251/800 9875
Contact Liz Davies
Fills the gap in the statutory services by providing crisis support and counselling for parents of critically ill children, especially those in intensive care. Provides 24-hour crisis line offering support and advice; when possible, meets parents at hospital

and offers mediation and communication between distressed parents and staff. Runs a bereavement counselling service.
C B V P

Parents of Murdered Children Support Group, Compassionate Friends

6 Denmark Street, Bristol BS1 5DQ
0272–292778
Contact Ann Robinson
A national self-help group for bereaved parents, offering understanding and emotional support via telephone calls and letters. In addition, can refer members to their local Victims Support Scheme.
C B V P

Parents of Parents Eternal Triangle – Grandparents and Children's Rights Group

15 Calder Close, Higher Compton, Plymouth PL3 6NT
0752–777036
Contact Shirley Hefferman
Aims to establish contact between grandparents and grandchildren who are denied access to each other through divorce, death of a parent, being taken into care etc. Provides advice and information to grandparents.
C B V P

Relate – National Marriage Guidance

Herbert Gray College, Little Church Street, Rugby, Warks CV21 3AP
0788–73241
Co-ordinates about 160 local Relate Centres (marriage guidance councils), which undertake education in personal relationships through discussions held in schools and youth clubs, as well as providing counselling for people seeking help in marriage and family relationships.
C B V P

Stillbirth and Neonatal Death Society

28 Portland Place, London W1N 4DE
01–436 5881
Contact Alison Howard
Offers support through self-help groups and befriending to bereaved parents who have suffered a still birth or neonatal death.
C B V P

Support in Gay Married Association

BM Sigma, London WC1N 3XX
01–837 7324
Contact Ask for Sigma Contact
Provides information and support for any heterosexual partner married to a homosexual partner.
V P

United Kingdom Marital Research Fund

Marriage Research Centre, Central Middlesex Hospital, Acton Lane, London NW10 7NS
01–965 2367/5733 ext 2309
Contact Janet Johns
Carries out research into marriage and family problems; provides a clinical service for couples.
C P

Westminster Carers Service

St James the Less Centre, Vauxhall Bridge Road, London SW1V 2PT
01–931 7440
Contact Jane Greenshields
Runs a free service allowing carers to have a break of up to 4 hours a week while their dependant is looked after by a replacement carer at home. May be able to advise on setting up a similar scheme in your locality.

SINGLE PARENTS AND STEP-PARENTS

Gingerbread

35 Wellington Street, London WC2E 7BN
01–240 0953
Provides support, help and social activities for lone parents and their children via a national network of mutual aid groups. Produces a wide range of literature to help lone parents.
C B V P

Holiday Endeavour for Lone Parents

52 Chequer Avenue, Hyde Park, Doncaster DN4 5AS
0302–65139
Contact D Cullingworth
Helps to provide low cost holidays for single-parent families in the UK.
C V P

KIDIHOLS

see p.33

National Council for One-Parent Families

255 Kentish Town Road, London NW5 2LX
01–267 1361
Contact Christine Nickles
Works to improve the financial, legal and social position of Britain's 957,000 one-parent families. Offers free, confidential help and advice to any one-parent family on any problem. Campaigns on a wide range of legal and welfare issues affecting one-parent families.
C P

SPLASH – Single Parent Links and Special Holidays

19 North Street, Plymouth, Devon PL4 9AH
Contact Jane King
Arranges low-cost holidays for single-

parent families and unaccompanied children.
C V P

Stepfamily – National Stepfamily Association
162 Tenison Road, Cambridge
CB1 2DP
0223–460312
Contact Richard Hodder
Provides advice, information and counselling service for stepfamilies; runs local self-help groups.
C B V P

ORGANISATIONS OFFERING ADVICE ON SPECIFIC TOPICS
FINANCIAL AND LEGAL
Action for Benefits
124–130 Southwark Street, London
SE1 0TU
01–928 9671 ext 257
Contact Linzi Taylor
Campaigns for an improved system of Social Security benefits; distributes information about current DHSS benefits; organises meetings and conferences; provides speakers for local groups.
B V P

Campaign Against Racist Laws
56 Edithna Street, London SW9 9JP
01–733 8508
Can give assistance to parents and children facing threat of deportation.

Charity Projects Ltd
47 Dean Street, London W1V 5HL
01–287 0833
Contact Grants Director
Innovative fund-raising charity; raises money to help young people who have problems with homelessness, drugs or alcohol misuse, or disability. Can offer free fundraising advice within their experience to charitable

groups sharing similar aims, through its Trust Fund.
C V

Children's Legal Centre
20 Compton Terrace, London N1 2UN
01–359 6251
Runs a free advice and information service by letter and telephone (2 – 5 pm weekdays) on all matters relating to children and the law. Publishes detailed information sheets on particular topics.
C V P

Family Rights Group
6–9 Manor Gardens, Holloway Road, London N7 6LA
01–263 4016/9724 (except Tues am)
Advice line **01–272 7308** (Mon, Wed, Fri 9.30–12.30)
Offers advice to families with children in public care or involved in child protection procedures. Holds up-to-date information about local self-help groups in Britain.
C P

Federation of Claimants' Unions
296 Bethnal Green Road, London
E2 0AG
01–739 4173
Contact Percy Shelley
Campaigns for an adequate income for all people; especially for unemployed people. Local groups advise on welfare benefits rights.
B V P

Free Representation Unit
13 Gray's Inn Square, London
WC1R 5JP
01–831 0692
Provides free representation (to people who do not have means to pay) before a variety of tribunals, including Industrial and Social Security Appeals Tribunals and Immigration Adjudication hearings. Cases must be referred by another agency such as

Citizens Advice Bureau.
C V

Housing Debtline
The Birmingham Settlement,
318 Summer Lane, Birmingham
B19 3RL
021–359 8501/2/3/4
Contact Jeff Brown/Simon Johnson
Aims to try and prevent
homelessness by giving advice which
helps people to combat rent and
mortgage arrears, taking into
consideration the caller's financial
position and other debts. Runs a
telephone helpline; offers practical
and legal advice.
C P

International Social Service of Great Britain
Cranmer House, 39 Brixton Road,
London SW9 6DD
01–735 9841
Contact Director
Aims to give a casework service to
help British, Commonwealth, foreign,
refugee or stateless people whose
personal and family problems extend
across national frontiers. Runs a
foreign marriage advisory service.
C V

Joint Council for the Welfare of Immigrants
115 Old Street, London EC1V 9JR
01–251 8706
Contact Sue Shutter
Advises, helps and represents
individuals and families facing
problems caused by the British
immigration and nationality laws.
B P

Justice for Children
35 Wellington Street, London
WC2 7BN
01–836 5917
Campaigns for the creation of family
courts to deal with all civil legal

matters relating to children and
parents. Runs advice and information
service for children, parents, social
workers and lawyers.
P

Minority Rights Group
29 Craven Street, London WC2N 5NT
01–930 6659
Campaigning organisation, concerned
to secure justice for groups suffering
from discrimination. Runs an
educational programme on human
and minority rights issues in UK
schools aimed at teachers and
students, and produces research
reports as well as educational
materials for use in the classroom.
C P

National Association of Citizens Advice Bureaux
115–123 Pentonville Road, London
N1 9LZ
01–833 2181
Contact Dominic Byrne
CABx provide free, impartial and
confidential advice and help to anyone
on any subject.
C B V P

Release
169 Commercial Street, London
E1 6BW
01–377 5905 (office); **01–603 8654**
(24-hour emergency)
Gives advice on drug-related legal
problems and emergency help in
cases of arrest.
P

Runnymede Trust
11 Princelet Street, London E1 6QH
01–375 1496
Contact Information Office
A research organisation concerned to
eliminate racism and injustice; will
answer questions on race or
immigration topics.
C P

United Kingdom Immigrants Advisory Service

County House, 190 Great Dover Street, London SE1 4YB
01–357 6917
Contact Information Officer
Offers advice to overseas nationals and Commonwealth citizens, including divided families, separated spouses and children, with a wide range of immigration and refugee problems; can represent them before immigration appeals adjudicators and tribunals.
C

HOUSING AND HOMELESS

Alone in London Service Ltd

West Lodge, I90 Euston Road, London NW1 2EF
01–387 6184 (head office) **01–278 4228** (advice and counselling service)
Assists young single homeless people by providing advice, counselling and accommodation.

Carematch Residential Care Consortium

see under HANDICAP, p.56

Caribbean Community Centre

416 Seven Sisters Road, Manor House, London N4 2LX
01–802 0550
Contact Sister Joseph Harding
May be able to offer accommodation and counselling for homeless black young people adrift in London; provides a wide range of educational, recreational and pastoral services for black young people in the north London area.
C V P

Carr-Gomm Society Ltd

38 Gomm Road, London SE16 2TX
01–231 9284
Contact Referrals Section
Provides small permanent homes for lonely men and women of any age with various social or personal problems; sponsors local societies with similar aims throughout the UK.
C B V P

Catholic Housing Aid Society

189a Old Brompton Road, London SW5 0AR
01–373 4961
Contact Robina Rafferty
Local groups can give free advice to any families in housing need.
C B V P

Centrepoint Soho

33 Long Acre, London WC2 9LA
01–379 3466
Runs night shelter in central London for young people (under 19); provides emergency and long-stay accommodation for homeless young people in London. Publishes 'Survival Guide' for young people.
C V P

CHAR, Housing Campaign for Single People

5–15 Cromer Street, London WC1H 8LS
01–833 2071
A campaigning organisation, but also works to help young homeless single people, especially those who have drifted to big cities, or who have experienced discrimination on grounds of race, colour, sex or sexual orientation. Publishes practical guides.
P

Church Housing Association Ltd

Weldford House, 112a Shirland Road, London W9 2BT
01–289 2241
Aims to provide housing for people who are homeless or unsatisfactorily housed, and for whom no other alternative exists. Currently provides over 2,500 family homes.
C B

Federation of Private Residents Associations

11 Dartmouth Street, London
SW1H 9BL
01–222 0037
Helps set up tenants'/ lessees'/
residents' associations in privately
rented blocks of flats or conversions;
provides information and legal advice
to member associations only.
P

First Key

Hartley House, Green Walk, London
SE1 4TV
01–378 7441
Works with local authority social
services and voluntary agencies to
help improve policy and practice with
regard to young people leaving care.
Provides information and advice.
C B P

Girls Alone Project

76 Oakley Square, London NW1 1WH
01–387 7801
Contact Beverley Lynch
Runs a hostel for homeless single
women under 19, in which they can
learn to take responsibility for their
own lives and also learn the skills
necessary for independent living. Girls
have to be referred by a social work
professional.
C B

Habinteg Housing Association Ltd

10 Nottingham Place, London
W1M 3FL
01–935 6931
Contact Housing Management
Department
A specialist housing association,
which concentrates on providing
accommodation for people in the
greatest housing need. Builds
specially-designed homes for
wheelchair users and their families,
integrated with the community.
C P

Housing Debtline

see p.44

Leaving Home Project

5 Egmont House, 116 Shaftesbury
Avenue, London W1V 7DJ
01–437 2068
Works to increase public knowledge
and awareness, especially among
young people, of the problems of
housing and homelessness, and the
difficulties that can arise when leaving
home. Produces educational
materials; runs an advisory service
and training courses.
C P

Piccadilly Advice Centre

100 Shaftesbury Avenue, London
W1V 7DH
01–434 3773 (advice); **01–437 1579**
(administration)
Contact Jayne Egerton
Provides advice and information to
people experiencing difficulties with
housing, especially young people;
provides information on local and
specialist advice services to enquirers
from all over the country.
C P

Shelter – National Campaign for the Homeless

88 Old Street, London EC1V 9HU
01–253 0202
Contact Information Office
Works to relieve poverty and distress
among the homeless.
C B V P

Simon Community

PO Box 1187, London NW5 4HW
Provides a variety of services for all
people (young and adult) sleeping
rough, including street-work and
medical care.
C V

Stonham Housing Association Ltd
Octavia House, 54 Ayres Street,
London SE1 1EU
01–403 1144
Contact Housing Services Advisory
Officer
Provides housing for disadvantaged
people, including ex-offenders, the
families of people in custody, single-
parent families, abused wives, and
children coming out of care.
C B

LESBIAN AND GAY

Lesbian Custody Project, Rights of Women
Rights of Women (LC), 52–54
Featherstone Street, London
EC1Y 8RT
01–251 6576
Contact Lesbian Custody Worker
Gives advice, information and support
to women involved in child custody
disputes where lesbianism is an
issue. Can refer parents to
experienced legal professionals. Can
put isolated lesbian mothers and their
children in contact with others.
B V P

Lesbian and Gay Youth Movement
BM/GYM, London WC1N 3XX
01–317 9690
Offers advice, support and
information to lesbians and gay men
under 26 years of age, including a
telephone helpline service.
B V P

London Lesbian and Gay Switchboard
Box BM Switchboard, London
WC1N 3XX
01–837 7324
Contact Costa Leontarkis
Provides a telephone information,
counselling and referral service for

homosexual men and lesbians.
Provides information to schools,
colleges, social services departments,
concerned parents etc.
V

Support in Gay Married Association
see p.42

OTHER

Escalator Safety Action Group
81 Mulberry Road, Bourneville,
Birmingham B30 1SX
021–495 0409
A campaigning group, concerned to
warn the public in general, and
parents of young children in particular,
of the dangers that are inherent in all
escalators.
V

National Campaign for Firework Reform
15, 118 Long Acre, London
WC2E 9PA
01–836 6703
Contact Dudley Savill
A pressure group campaigning to
restrict the sale of fireworks to
licensed people over the age of 18, so
as to reduce the number of deaths
and injuries caused by fireworks.
B V P

Suzy Lamplugh Trust
14 East Sheen Avenue, London
SW14 8AS
01–392 1839
Contact Elaine Bishop
Can give talks to mothers, children
and school groups on the avoidance of
potentially dangerous situations.
C V P

Victims' Help Line
see under HEALTH, p.63

HANDICAP

MENTAL HANDICAP

GENERAL

Association for Brain-Damaged Children

Clifton House, 3 St Paul's Road, Foleshill, Coventry CV6 5DE
0203–56517
Contact Rose Bennett
Provides short-term respite care and holiday scheme for handicapped children; gives help, support and advice to their parents, runs a domiciliary speech therapy service for handicapped and pre-school children.
C V P

Association of Residential Communities for the Retarded

The Old Rectory, Church Lane North, Old Whittington, Chesterfield
S41 9QY
0246–455881
Contact James Churchill
An umbrella charity for organisations providing residential care for people with learning difficulties. Its members provide about 7000 bed spaces in residential homes nationwide.

British Institute of Mental Handicap

Wolverhampton Road, Kidderminster, DY10 3DD
0562–850251
Administers and runs training courses; maintains a resources centre and library for use by members; produces publications.
C P

Campaign for People with Mental Handicaps

12a Maddox Street, London W1R 9PL
01–491 0727
Contact Steve Dowson
Works to further the rights of mentally-handicapped people, and to ensure that their conditions of life are as close as possible to those of non-handicapped people. Can provide information about latest research findings and new ideas.
C B P

Camphill Village Trust Ltd

Delrow House, Aldenham, Watford, Herts WD2 8DJ
0923–856006
Contact Ann Harris MBE
Provides a home, work, education and general care for long-stay mentally-handicapped adults in village communities. Runs counselling service, publicity and fundraising campaigns.
C B P

CARE for Mentally-Handicapped People

9a Weir Road, Kibworth, Leicester LE8 0LO
Contact J E Higgins
Runs residential communities for mentally-handicapped men and women; provides care, support, guidance and training as appropriate.

Caring and Sharing

Cottons Farmhouse, Whiston Road, Cogenhoe, Northants NN7 1NL
Contact Caroline Scattergood

Provides help, support and advice to mentally-handicapped people and their parents, particularly those living in rural areas.
C P

Children's Aid Team
75/77 Granville Road, London N22 5LX
01–888 4189
Provides help for mentally-handicapped people and their families, including a 24-hour crisis service.
C B V P

Christian Concern for the Mentally Handicapped
PO Box 351, Reading, Berks RG1 7AL
Contact Tony Phelps-Jones
Runs residential care homes for people with mental handicaps.
C V

L'Arche Ltd
14 London Road, Beccles, Suffolk NR34 9NH
0502–715329
Contact M B Hollis
Runs community homes and workshops where people with mental handicaps and assistants can share life together.

MacIntyre
2 Ridgeway Court, Grovebury Road, Leighton Buzzard, Beds LU7 8SW
0525–370102
Contact John Thorne
Provides long-term care, education and occupations for mentally-handicapped children and adults.
C V P

Mencap *see* Royal Society for Mentally Handicapped Children and Adults

National Federation of Gateway Clubs
117 Golden Lane, London EC1Y 0RT
01–253 9433
Contact Marian O'Mara
Runs a network of social, recreational and educational clubs for mentally-handicapped young people. Runs training courses for leaders and helpers. Maintains links with other youth organisations.
B V P

One-to-One
33 Cornelia Street, London N7 8BA
01–607 8327
Contact Jean Wilson
Arranges a series of practical projects, including volunteer tutoring, advocacy, arts and drama, for mentally-handicapped people in long-stay hospitals.

Ravenswood Foundation
221 Golders Green Road, London NW11 9DZ
01–458 3282
Contact Julian Sorsby
Provides residential care for mentally-handicapped children, various welfare services, a training scheme and a hospital visiting scheme.
C B V

Royal Society for Mentally Handicapped Children and Adults (MENCAP)
Mencap National Centre, 123 Golden Lane, London EC1Y 0RT
01–253 9433
Contact Hasu Morar
Offers advice, information and services to support mentally-handicapped people, in conjunction with over 550 local societies. Services include residential homes, leisure activities, employment placement, training, specialist legal advice and voluntary welfare visitors.
C B V P

United Kingdom Sports Association for People with a Mental Handicap

Unit 9, Longlands Industrial Estate, Milner Way, Ossett WF5 9JN
0924–280027
Contact Mark Southam
An umbrella organisation for sport for people with a mental handicap in the UK. Can provide information about local clubs and facilities.
C B V P

SPECIFIC CONDITIONS

Association of Parents of Vaccine-Damaged Children

2 Church Street, Shipston-on-Stour, Warks CV36 4AP
0608–61595
Campaigns for a government compensation scheme which will provide for the needs of vaccine-damaged children for the rest of their lives.
V

Down's Syndrome Association

12–13 Clapham Common Southside, London SW4 7AA
01–720 0008
Contact Lee Baker
A parents' self-help organisation, concerned with the care, nurture and education of all people with Down's Syndrome, particularly in the early years of life. Provides advice and information.
C B V P

International Autistic Research Organisation

49 Orchard Avenue, Shirley, Croydon CR0 7NE
01–777 0095 (24 hours)
Contact G M McCarthy
Raises funds for research into this condition; answers enquiries from parents and the general public. Undertakes research studies.
C V P

National Autistic Society

276 Willesden Lane, London NW2 5RB
01–451 1114
Contact Information Officer
Provides and promotes day and residential centres for the care and education of autistic children and adults. Runs an advisory and information service together with regular courses and conferences. Maintains links with local affiliated societies and encourages research.
C B V P

ORGANISATIONS FOR PEOPLE WITH VARIOUS DISABILITIES

ADVICE AND INFORMATION

Association for Stammerers

c/o The Finsbury Centre, Pine Street, London EC1R 0JH
Contact Nina Parkhouse
Promotes self-help, disseminates information and sponsors research. Links individual stammerers with existing groups, and encourages the formation of new groups.
C V P

British Council of Organisations of Disabled People

St Mary's Church, Greenlaw Street, London SE18 5AR
01–316 4184
Contact Anne Rae
Encourages links between new and existing self-help groups for disabled people; can provide information about local groups to enquirers.
C B V

British Institute for Brain-Injured Children

Knowle Hall, Knowle, Bridgewater, Somerset TA7 8PJ
0278–684060

Contact M Coulson
Can prescribe treatment programmes for brain-injured children to be carried out at home by parents and volunteers.
C V P

Carers National Association
29 Chilworth Mews, London W2 3RG
01–724 7776
Offers information and advice to carers (people who care for someone who is mentally ill, mentally or physically handicapped, or chronically unwell); puts carers in touch with others in similar circumstances.

Disability Alliance
25 Denmark Street, London WC2H 8NJ
01–240 0806
Contact Linda Lennard
Campaigning organisation trying to persuade society to pay an income as of right to all disabled persons on equitable principles according to the severity of their disability. A sister organisation, Disability Alliance Educational and Research Trust (same address) runs a welfare rights service and produces publications on the social security system for people with disabilities and their families.
C V P

Disabled Christians Fellowship
50 Clare Road, Kingswood, Bristol BS15 1PJ
0272–616141
Promotes social links and Christian fellowship between members of the group; runs Teens and Twenties section for young disabled people.
C B V P

Disablement Income Group
Millmead Business Centre, Millmead Road, London N17 9QU
01–801 8013
Contact Margaret Lavery

Campaigns to improve the financial welfare of all disabled people; offers advice on welfare benefits to disabled people.
C B P

In Touch
10 Norman Road, Sale, Cheshire M33 3DF
061–962 4441
Contact Ann Worthington
Provides informal contacts between parents of children with rare disabilities to enable them to offer and receive support and to exchange ideas and information.
C P

Invalid Children's Aid Nationwide
198 City Road, London EC1V 2PH
01–608 2462
Provides free help and advice for parents with disabled children, to help them live as full a life as possible regardless of the type of disability. Runs an information service, special schools, and a further education college. Produces a wide range of publications.
C B V P

Invalids at Home
17 Lapstone Gardens, Kenton, Harrow HA3 0EB
01–907 1706
Contact Sarah Lomas
Aims to help permanent invalids to leave hospital or to live at home by making grants for equipment and other needs at the request of social workers. Covers all ages and disabilities.
C V

John Grooms's Association for the Disabled
10 Gloucester Drive, London N4 2LP
01–802 7272
Contact C Moore
Runs a large number of projects to

help physically-disabled people throughout England and Wales, including residential accommodation, family holiday schemes, housing and information services.
C B V P

Kith and Kids
see under FAMILY WELFARE, p.33

Mobility Information Service
National Mobility Service, Unit 2a Atcham Estate, Shrewsbury, SY4 4UG
074375–889
Contact Jean Griffiths
Provides a mobility advisory and information service for disabled people and those who work with them.
V P

National Association of Disablement Information Advice Lines
Victoria Buildings, 117 High Street, Clay Cross, Chesterfield, Derbyshire S45 9DZ
0246–250055
Contact Beryl Redwood
Provides a free, impartial and confidential information service for disabled people; advice is supplied by people with direct personal experience of disability through local groups.
C B V P

National Council for Special Education
1 Wood Street, Stratford upon Avon, Warks CV37 6JE
0789–204332
Aims to further the education and welfare of all people who are in any way handicapped.
C B V P

National Federation of St Raphael Clubs
100 Southland, Swaffham, Norfolk PE37 7PG
0760–21422
Contact Ernest J Richardson
Co-ordinates the activities of a network of clubs for disabled people in south-east England. May be able to advise on setting up similar clubs in other regions. Can supply information on technical aids, household equipment etc.
C B V

Network for the Handicapped
16 Princeton Street, London WC1R 4BB
01–831 8031/7740
Contact Helen Berent
Gives legal advice, assistance and information to handicapped people and their families.
C V

Outset
Drake House, 18 Creekside, London SE8 3DZ
01–692 7141
Undertakes surveys into the needs of disabled people; runs training and employment projects for people with disabilities involving computerised office skills (London area).
C P B

Parents with Disabilities Group (an offshoot of the National Childbirth Trust)
9 Queenborough Terrace, London W2 3TB
Contact Jo O'Farrell, 6 Forest Road, Crowthorne, Berks RG11 7EH, 0344–773366
Provides information, help and support to parents and prospective parents with disabilities. Maintains a national register of parents with disabilities who are willing to give

advice and help to new parents.
C B V P

Skill – National Bureau for Students with Disabilities

336 Brixton Road, London SW9 7AA
01–274 0565
Contact Deborah Cooper
Works to develop opportunities in further, higher and adult education, training and employment for young people and adults with special educational and training needs throughout the UK. Can provide information to individual students and their parents.
C B P

Special Equipment and Aids for Living (SEQUAL)

Ddol Hir, Glyn Ceriog, Llangollen, Clwyd LL20 7NP
Contact Linda Aldridge
Provides communication aids and a welfare assessment service for the profoundly disabled.
C B V

SPOD (Association to Aid Sexual and Personal Relationships of People with a Disability)

286 Camden Road, London N7 0BJ
01–607 8851/2
Contact Information Officer
Provides information and advice on the problems in sex and personal relationships which disability can cause.
C P

PARTICULAR ACTIVITIES

Association of Swimming Therapy

4 Oak Street, Shrewsbury SY3 7RH
0743–4393
Contact Ted Cowen
Organises national and regional galas; publishes numerous training videos. Teaches swimming to handicapped people of all ages and with all

disabilities. Maintains contact among local clubs. Gives demonstrations and runs training courses.
C B V P

British Sports Association for the Disabled

Haward House, Barnard Crescent, Aylesbury, Bucks HP21 9PP
Provides opportunities for people with a mental or physical handicap to take part in all forms of recreation and sport. Maintains development officers working in all the Sports Council regions.
C B V P

Camping for the Disabled

20 Burton Close, Dawley, Telford, Shropshire TF4 2BX
0743–77489
Contact Maurice Stockton
Offers information and advice on camping for disabled people and supplies details of adapted sites for campers in Britain and Europe. Arranges summer weekend camps for disabled people in the UK.
P

Catholic Handicapped Fellowship

2 The Villas, Hare Law, Stanley, Co Durham DH9 8DQ
0207–234397
Contact M M Donnelly
Can put parents of handicapped children in touch with their local Diocesan representative; each diocese of the Fellowship arranges a variety of educational, recreational and welfare activities for handicapped people of all ages.
C B V

Creative Young People Together

Forum, Stirling Road, Chichester, West Sussex PO19 2EN
Contact Gillian Purvis
Provides short-term, residential arts workshops for young (18–30) people

with disabilities; outreach work on arts and disability, especially among the young.
C B V

Disabled Photographers' Society

190 Secrett House, Ham Close, Ham, Richmond, Surrey TW10 7PE
01–948 2342
Provides help, advice, and specially-adapted equipment to disabled people, including children, interested in photography. Special help given to schools.
C

Federation to Promote Horticulture for Disabled People

9 Miles Close, Yapton, West Sussex BN18 0TB
0903–72401
Can provide information about organisations concerned with encouraging disabled adults and children to enjoy and benefit from horticulture.
C P

Gardens for the Disabled Trust and Garden Club

Old House Farm, Peasmarsh, Rye, East Sussex TN31 6YD
079721–286
Contact Susan van Laun
Provides practical and financial assistance to disabled people wishing to take an active part in gardening. Offers advice to individuals, institutions, schools, hospitals.
C V P

Great Britain Wheelchair Basketball Association

c/o 16 Atkinson Road, Sale, Cheshire M33 1FY
061–230 7462
Contact Tony Sainsbury
Encourages and promotes the sport of wheelchair basketball.
C B V

Handicapped Adventure Playground Association

Fulham Palace, Bishop's Avenue, London SW6 6EA
01–736 4443
Maintains adventure playgrounds in the London area; offers a national information service to individuals and groups wanting to set up adventure playgrounds in their own localities.

Handicapped Aid Trust

Eskdale, 47 Aldenham Avenue, Radlett, Herts WD7 8HZ
01–900 2151
Contact Janet Marshall, 21 Malden Hill, New Malden, Surrey KT3 4DS
Makes grants towards the costs of helpers to accompany severely-handicapped people on holiday, where these costs cannot be met by the holidaymaker.
C

Handicapped Anglers Trust

29 Ironlatch Avenue, St Leonard's on Sea, East Sussex TN38 9JE
0424–427931
Contact L D Warren
Encourages handicapped people to participate in angling; provides advice and information.
C B V

Handicapped Children's Pilgrimage Trust and Hosanna House Trust

100a High Street, Banstead, Surrey SM7 2RB
0737–353311
Contact Paul Chitnis
Assists disabled and disadvantaged children to make a pilgrimage to Lourdes, and provides voluntary medical and nursing helpers to accompany them. Arranges accommodation for other disabled people at a specially-adapted house in Lourdes.
C B V

Horticultural Therapy
Goulds Ground, Vallis Way, Frome,
Somerset BA11 3DW
0373–64782
Contact Ray Williams
Promotes and encourages the use of
horticulture, agriculture and gardening
in therapy, rehabilitation, vocational
training, leisure, education and useful
employment for people with all kinds
of disability, handicap or
disadvantage. Maintains local groups.
C B V P

Mobility International
228 Borough High Street, London
SE1 1JX
01–403 5688
Contact Anthony Lumley
Aims to promote the integration into
society of people who are in any way
handicapped, through international
travel and exchange. Runs a variety of
programmes, including youth festivals
and young people's activity schemes.
P

Music for the Disabled
2 Wendy Crescent, Guildford, Surrey
GU2 6RP
0483–67813
Contact Gwenyth Malby
Arranges for concerts of live music, or
for the loan of cassette tapes etc, to
physically- and mentally- disabled
people of all ages in hospitals,
schools, clubs etc, or as
entertainment and therapy for
disabled children. At present operates
in Surrey and Sussex only, but hopes
to extend. May be able to advise on
setting up similar schemes locally.
B V

National Association of Swimming Clubs for the Handicapped
The Old Tea House, The Square,
Wickham, Hants PO17 5JT
The national co-ordinating body for
swimming clubs for handicapped
people. Aims to encourage, promote
and develop swimming among
handicapped people. Can provide
parents with details of a club near
them.
C B V P

Paget Gorman Society
3 Gipsy Lane, Headington, Oxford
OX3 7PT
0865–61908
Contact R G Newby
Helps children and young people
suffering from speech and language
handicaps to communicate and
develop language skills through the
use of Paget Gorman Signed Speech.
Part of Invalid Children's Aid
Nationwide.
C B V P

Radio Amateur Invalid and Blind Club
9 Conigre, Chinnor, Oxon OX9 4JY
0844–51461
Contact Cathy Clark
Assists disabled radio amateurs and
shortwave listeners; organises
nationwide groups; raises funds;
loans equipment to members.
B V

Riding for the Disabled Association
Avenue R, National Agricultural
Centre, Kenilworth, Warks CV8 2LY
0203–696510
Contact J Moss
Provides the opportunity to ride or
drive for disabled children and adults;
local groups throughout the UK.
C B V P

Young Disabled on Holiday
6 Yewland Drive, Boothsmere,
Knutsford, Cheshire WA16 8AP
Contact Rosemary Girdlestone
Organises and facilitates holidays for
young disabled people aged 18–30.
C V P

SERVICES

National Library for the Handicapped Child
see under EDUCATION, p.10

Sue Ryder Foundation
Cavendish, Suffolk CO10 8AY
0787–280252
Contact Information Officer
Maintains a network of homes to care for sick and disabled people, including the mentally ill.
C V

Tadworth Court Trust
Tadworth Court Children's Hospital, Tadworth, Surrey KT20 5RU
0737–357171
Contact Information Officer
Aims to assist in the provision of care, treatment, rehabilitation and relief for sick, physically- and/or mentally-handicapped children; maintains a variety of services, including Tadworth Court Children's Hospital and St Margaret's School. Also provides short-term respite care for profoundly handicapped children, a rehabilitation service for children with head injuries, and hospice care.
C V P

Talking Books Library
12 Lant Street, London SE1 1QH
01–407 9417
Contact Marylyn Rayner
Provides a postal lending service of literature recorded on cassettes for physically- and mentally-handicapped adults and children who are unable to read in the conventional way.
Dyslexics are also eligible.
C V P

PHYSICAL HANDICAP
GENERAL

Carematch Residential Care Consortium
286 Camden Road, London N7 0BJ
01–609 9966
Contact Jackie Higginson
Runs a computerised matching and counselling service for physically-disabled people looking for residential accommodation.
C

Centre on Environment for the Handicapped
35 Great Smith Street, London SW1P 3BJ
01–222 7980
Contact Tessa Palfreyman
Aims to inform architects and other professionals of the needs of disabled people. Can advise parents on altering or adapting their home to make it accessible to children with disabilities, and put parents in touch with local architects who have experience of designing for disabled people.
C V P

Disabled Housing Trust
Ernest Kleinwort Court, Oakenfield, Burgess Hill, West Sussex RH15 8SJ
Contact Brenda Kay
Offers specialist housing and residential care homes for physically-handicapped people and their families, offering them a lifestyle that is equal to that enjoyed by their able-bodied counterparts.
C B

Disabled Living Foundation
380–384 Harrow Road, London W9 2HU
01–289 6111
Runs an information service and a reference library for people of all ages with any disability, an incontinence advisory service, a clothing advisory

service, an equipment centre, advisory services for music and visual handicap, and for footwear/footcare. Exhibition of equipment and the library may be visited by appointment.
C V P

Lady Hoare Trust for Physically Disabled Children

Alma Lodge, 75 Alma Road, Windsor, Berks SL4 3HD
0753–830508
Contact Lillian Ramsay
Cares for physically-disabled children and their families, especially those suffering from Juvenile Chronic Arthritis, through its nationwide team of professionally qualified social workers.
C B P

Leonard Cheshire Foundation

Leonard Cheshire House, 26–29 Maunsel Street, London SW1P 2QN
01–828 1822
Contact W J Sullivan
Maintains over 78 Cheshire Homes in the UK, catering for severely physically-disabled men and women. There is limited provision for mentally-handicapped children and adults. Also runs Family Support Services, which offer part-time help to handicapped people living at home and their families, and a country house hotel for disabled people.
C B V P

Mobility Trust

4 Hughes Mews, 143a Chatham Road, London SW11 6HJ
01–924 3597
Contact Peter Mahon
Runs educational and day centres; loans or grants, special aids or equipment for people with disabilities.
C B V

PHAB (Physically Handicapped and Able-Bodied)

Tavistock House North (2nd Floor), Tavistock Square, London WC1H 9HX
01–388 1963
Works to further the integration of physically-handicapped people into the community. Runs over 450 clubs with a joint membership of physically handicapped and able bodied, plus holiday schemes.
C B V

Royal Association for Disability and Rehabilitation

25 Mortimer Street, London W1N 8AB
01–637 5400
Contact Alison Hibberd
Co-ordinates the activities of over 400 member associations with improving access, education, employment, holidays, housing and mobility for disabled people.
C B V P

SPECIFIC DISABILITIES

Association of Local Voluntary Organisations for the Deaf

Centre for the Deaf, 17 St Mary's Square, Gloucester GL1 2QT
0452–20747
Contact N J Bone
Co-ordinates information on local services for deaf people in different parts of the country.

Association for Spina Bifida and Hydrocephalus

22 Woburn Place, London WC1H 0EP
01–388 1382
Contact Monica Hart
Concerned to promote the care, welfare, interest, treatment, education and advancement of people suffering from spina bifida, hydrocephalus, and related conditions, and their families.

Maintains local branches throughout the country; offers information and advice; sponsors research.

Association for Spinal Injury Research, Rehabilitation and Reintegration (ASPIRE)

16 East Heath Road, London NW3 1AL
01–209 1072/01–209 0868
Contact Shannie Ross
Aims to finance research into the treatment of spinal chord injury, to promote the rehabilitation and integration into society of people with spinal injuries, and to educate the public about spinal injury prevention.
C B V P

Bobath Centre

5 Netherhall Gardens, London NW3 5RN
01–435 3895
Contact Simon Sheffield
Provides treatment for children suffering from cerebral palsy and allied neurological disorders; trains doctors and therapists and encourages research. British children treated free of charge must be referred by a consultant paediatrician.
C P

Breakthrough Trust, Deaf-Hearing Integration

Central Office, Charles W Gillet Centre, Selly Oak Colleges, Birmingham B29 6LE
021–471 4363 (Voice); 021–472 5488 (Vistel)
Aims to promote social and cultural activities which bring deaf and hearing people into contact through practical self-help ventures. Provides opportunities for children, families and individuals to become involved. Runs information service, parent/toddler groups, toy libraries, workshops.
C B V P

British Association of the Hard of Hearing

7–11 Armstrong Road, London W3 7JL
01–743 1110/1353
Contact J C Shaw
Helps to set up clubs and classes for people with impaired hearing; organises recreational and educational activities; encourages the practice of lip-reading.
C B V P

British Blind Sport

15B Bell Lane, Byfield, Daventry Northants NN11 6US
0372–62214
Contact Julie L Whiting
Provides opportunities for visually handicapped people to participate in sporting activities at all levels.
C B V P

British Deaf Association

38 Victoria Place, Carlisle, Cumbria, CA1 1HU
0228–48844
Campaigns on behalf of deaf people; awards grants and scholarships to further the education of deaf students; runs welfare programme for deaf people in special need. Provides advice on the education, fostering and adoption of deaf children.
C B V P

British Polio Fellowship

Bell Close, West End Road, Ruislip, Middx HA4 6LP
0895–675515
Contact Leo P Jackson
Offers support and welfare services for people suffering the after-effects of polio. Provides holiday and residential accommodation.
C B V P

Cleft Lip and Palate Association

1 Eastwood Gardens, Kenton,
Newcastle-upon-Tyne, NE3 3DQ
091–285 9396
Contact Cy Thirlaway
Supports families with children
affected by this condition; offers
advice, information and counselling.
C B P

Deaf Broadcasting Council

592 Kenilworth Road, Balsall
Common, Coventry CV7 7DQ
0203–832076
Acts as consumer body for deaf and
hard-of-hearing viewers. Makes
representations to broadcasting
authorities based on members'
opinions. Provides information to
members.
C B V P

Friends for the Young Deaf Trust

FYD Communications Centre, East
Court Mansion, Council Office,
College Lane, East Grinstead, West
Sussex RH19 3LT
0342–323444 (Voice); **0342–312639**
(Vistel Minicom)
Contact Morag Rosie
Promotes the well-being and social
education of the young deaf,
especially children and those from
under-privileged backgrounds. Runs
programme of recreational and
educational activities; leadership
courses for 14–25 year olds.
C B V P

Guide Dogs for the Blind Association

Alexandra House, 9 Park Street,
Windsor, Berks SL4 1JR
0753–855711
Contact Hugh McRoberts
Provides and trains guide dogs for
blind people over 16 years of age.
Raises funds to support this work.
C B V

Hearing Dogs for the Deaf

The Training Centre, London
Road(A40), Lewknor, Oxford OX9 5RY
0844–53898
Contact Doreen McInnes
Supplies trained dogs to assist
profoundly deaf and hard of hearing
people by alerting them by touch to
specific household sounds, and
provide them with companionship,
protection, mobility, and continued
support services.

Jewish Blind Society (incorporating The Jewish Association for the Physically Handicapped)

221 Golders Green Road, London
NW11 9DN
01–458 3282
Contact Anthony Krais
Aims to assist visually-handicapped
and also younger physically-disabled
people within the Jewish community.
Provides a variety of welfare,
residential and day care services.
C B V P

National Association for Limbless Disabled

31 The Mall, Ealing, London W5 2PX
01–579 1758/9
Contact Triona O'Loughlin
Promotes the welfare of limbless
people and assists in the rehabilitation
of recent amputees. Runs an advisory
service.
C B V P

National Deaf-Blind League

18 Rainbow Court, Paston Ridings,
Peterborough PE4 6UP
0733–73511
Contact Ann Barnett
Arranges social activities and contacts
by post for deaf-blind people;
provides material help for holidays,
equipment and sickness.
C B V P

National Deaf Children's Society

45 Hereford Road, London W2 5AH
01–229 9272 (voice); **01–229 1891**
(Vistel)
Contact Colin Redman
Works to obtain for deaf children the
best possible medical, audiological,
educational and health services and to
support deaf children's families. Gives
free advice, counselling and
information on all aspects of
childhood deafness. Runs the NDCS
Technology Information Centre to
give advice on new equipment and
aids: 021–454 5151 (voice); 021–454
9795 (Vistel).
C B V P

National Federation of the Blind in the UK

Unity House, Westgate, Wakefield,
W. Yorks WF1 1ER
Campaigns for the integration of
visually-handicapped children into
ordinary schools, and for an
improvement in the quality of life for
all blind people.
C B V P

National Library for the Blind

Cromwell Road, Bredbury, Stockport
SK6 2SG
061–494 0217
Contact Information Officer
Supplies books in braille and Moon,
also in large print. Services are free
and post-free to registered blind
people.
C P V

National Network of Deaf Students

c/o Bulmershe College of Higher
Education, Woodlands Avenue,
Earley, Reading RG6 1HY
0734–666506
Contact Craig A Crowley
Promotes the rights, needs and
interests of deaf students in further,
higher and continuing education.
V P

Partially Sighted Society

Queen's Road, Doncaster
Contact Jo Beech, 224 Great
Portland Street, London W1N 6AA
01–387 8840
Advises and assists partially-sighted
people; maintains a network of local
branches which offer contact and
support. Pioneers low vision training.
C B V P

REACH – the Association for Children with Hand or Arm Deficiency

13 Park Terrace, Crimchard, Chard,
Somerset TA20 1LA
0460–61578
Contact John Bruce
Works to improve the lives of children
with upper limb deficiencies, and to
encourage mutual aid and support
among their families. Provides
information about artificial limbs and
reports on new technology.
C B V P

Royal Association in aid of Deaf People

27 Old Oak Road, London W3 7SL
01–743 6187
Contact Rosemary Brotherhood
Offers help to people of all ages who
have had a hearing impediment from
birth or early childhood; provides
interpreters; offers help and advice
with practical problems; arranges
recreational and spiritual activities.
C B V P

Royal National Institute for the Blind

224 Great Portland Street, London
WIN 6AA
01–388 1266
Provides a wide range of services for
blind and visually-handicapped
children and adults, including schools
and colleges, an education advisory
service, careers advice, information
on equipment and benefits, braille and

tape libraries for students.
C B V P

Royal National Institute for the Deaf

105 Gower Street, London
WC1E 6AH
01–387 8033
Contact Sandra Hanafin
Works to improve conditions affecting the education, employment and general welfare of people who are deaf. Provides information and advice on equipment and technical devices.
P

SENSE (National Deaf-Blind and Rubella Association)

311 Grays Inn Road, London
WC1X 8PT
01–278 1005
Contact Parent Liaison Officer or Information Section
Provides information and support to families with deaf-blind and rubella handicapped children.
C B V P

Sole-Mates

46 Gordon Road, Chingford, London
E4 6BU
01–524 2423
Contact Ann Cross
Helps people with different-sized feet to find a partner with whom to exchange shoes.

Spastics Society

12 Park Crescent, London W1N 4EQ
01–636 5020
Contact Information Office
Provides information, advice, support and a wide range of educational services for people with cerebral palsy and their families.
C P

Spinal Injuries Association

Newpoint House, 76 St James's Lane, London N10 3DS

01–444 2121
Contact Mary Anne Tyrrell
Provides information and advice to people with spinal cord injuries and their families.
C P

Stars' Organisation for Spastics

12 Park Crescent, London W1N 4EQ
01–637 9681
Maintains homes for people with cerebral palsy or similar handicaps; runs a project to develop pre-school services and to train staff to help children under 5 and their families; fundraising.
C V P

STEPS – National Association for Families of Children with Congenital Abnormalities of the Lower Limbs

8 Princess Road, Urmston, Manchester M31 3SS
061–747 7014
Provides support, information and contact for families of children with these conditions; offers practical help and advice; liaises with local hospitals; maintains local branches.
C B V

Torch Trust for the Blind

Torch House, Hallaton, Market Harborough, Leics LE16 8UJ
085889–301
Contact Secretary
Provides Christian literature and fellowship for visually-handicapped people, including children.
C B V P

Voluntary Organisations Communication and Language

336 Brixton Road, London SW9 7AA
01–274 4029
Contact Information Officer
Provides support and link services for people with communication handicaps.
C B V P

HEALTH

GENERAL ORGANISATIONS
ADVICE, INFORMATION AND COUNSELLING

Action for Victims of Medical Accidents
24 Southwark Street, London
SE1 1TY
01–403 4744
Contact Arnold Simanowitz
Advises people who have suffered as a result of medical treatment, or the failure to give medical treatment, on their rights. Refers them to solicitors if appropriate. Maintains a panel of independent medical experts and experienced solicitors.
C

Chest, Heart and Stroke Association
Tavistock House North, Tavistock Square, London WC1H 9JE
01–387 3012
Helps people who suffer from chest, heart and stroke illnesses; offers rehabilitation and welfare advice, and counselling.
C B V P

Health Information Trust
18 Victoria Park Square, London
E2 9PF
01–980 6263
Runs Healthline, a free, confidential telephone information service about health (2 pm – 10pm daily), and a 24-hour phone enquiry line about AIDS.
C P

Hospice Information Service
St Christopher's Hospice, 51–59 Lawrie Park Road, Sydenham, London SE26 6DZ
01–778 9252 ext 262/263
Contact Information Officer
Can provide information about the availability of hospice services in your area; publishes a Directory of Hospices in the UK.
C V

In Touch
see under HANDICAP, p.51

National Register for Rare Diseases – Share-a-Care
8 Cornmarket, Faringdon, Oxon
Contact J Braithwaite
Puts people with rare diseases (or their families) in contact with others with the same disorder. Runs a postal enquiries service.

Samaritans
17 Uxbridge Road, Slough, Berks
SL1 1SN
0753–32713
Helps suicidal and despairing people of all ages; runs a 24-hour, confidential telephone helpline service.
C B V P

Steroid Aid Group
PO Box 220, London E17 3JR
Contact Christopher Whatcott (0527–32671)/Babs Diplock (0472–696722)
Seeks information about steroid drugs and their side effects; campaigns for

improved public education; arranges contact between members for mutual help and advice.
B V P

Vegan Society

33–35 George Street, Oxford OX1 2AY
0865–722166
Contact Barry Kew
Can provide information on nutrition and on a vegan way of life.
C V P

Vegetarian Society of the United Kingdom Ltd

Parkdale, Dunham, Altrincham, Cheshire WA14 4QG
061–928 0793
Contact Information Officer
Can provide information on nutrition and on the vegetarian way of life. Also runs Youth Education Department to provide help and information to parents whose children wish to become vegetarians.
C B V P

Victims' Help Line

St Leonard's, Nuttall Street, London N1 5LZ
01–729 1226 (office); **01–729 1252** (24-hour helpline)
Offers a confidential helpline for any victim of any crime; provides counselling, advice, information and referral service.
C V

Westminster Pastoral Foundation

23 Kensington Square, London W8 5HN
01–937 6956
Provides a national counselling service for people with emotional, psychological, marital or family problems.
C B P

CAMPAIGNING AND PROMOTING HEALTH

British Heart Foundation

102 Gloucester Place, London W1H 4DH
01–935 0185
Contact Elaine Snell
Encourages and finances research; provides advice and information; produces educational materials to alert the public to the risks of heart disease; maintains 500 local groups.
C B V P

Campaign Against Lead in Petrol

171 Barnett Wood Lane, Ashtead, Surrey KT21 2LD
03722–75977
Contact Reg Mayes
Campaigns against lead pollution, especially that caused by lead in petrol and motor vehicle exhaust emissions; provides information for parents and children, research data, parliamentary briefings. Can supply speakers.
C V P

Corda, the Heart Charity

Tavistock House North, Tavistock Square, London WC1H 9TH
01–387 9779
Contact Sheila James
A fundraising body to support and promote specialist research into the prevention of heart and arterial disease; setting up local network of Friends of Corda.
C B V

Coronary Prevention Group

60 Great Ormond Street, London WC1N 3HR
01–833 3687
Provides information and educational materials to professionals and the general public to encourage measures to prevent coronary heart disease.

Advice given to parents on healthy eating and exercise for children and adults, on discouraging smoking and on improving school meals.
C P V

Good Practices in Mental Health

380–384 Harrow Road, London W9 2HU
01–289 2034/3060
Contact Yvonne Latawiec
Promotes the development of better mental health services through local studies, local development work and by spreading information about innovations in treatment and care. Runs an information service for mental health and social services planners, and other key professionals in the field.
C V P

Health Rights Ltd

344 South Lambeth Road, London SW8 1UQ
01–720 9811
Contact Beverley Beech
A group representing users of the National Health Service which works to improve maternity services, among other aims. Offers advice on women's rights during pregnancy and on the use of obstetric technology. Produces information booklets, undertakes research, runs seminars which are open to the public.
V P

Medic-Alert Foundation

11–13 Clifton Terrace, London N4 3JP
01–263 8596/7
An emergency protection scheme; the Medic-Alert emblem gives immediate help to police, ambulance and medical personnel and warns them of a child's or adult's hidden allergy or medical condition. A single payment gives life protection.
C

MIND

22 Harley Street, London W1N 2ED
01–637 0741; publications enquiries **01–387 9126**
Campaigning organisation, working to promote mental health and to help people with mental disorders; supports the work of over 200 local mental health organisations throughout the UK. Offers advice and a legal casework service.
C B V P

National Rubella Council

33–39 St Pancras Road, London NW1 2QB
01–837 0623
Contact Jenny Fieldgrass
Campaigns to encourage vaccination against rubella for women and girls, and to advertise the dangers of rubella during pregnancy. Encourages women and girls to take a more positive attitude towards their own health. Also supports the new measles/mumps/rubella (MMR) vaccine.
C

National Society for Clean Air

136 North Street, Brighton BN1 1RG
0273–26313
Contact Information Officer
Provides advice, information and educational materials about air pollution and noise.
C B P

ALCOHOL AND DRUG ABUSE

Accept Services UK

Accept Clinic, 200 Seagrove Road, London SW6 1RQ
01–381 3155
Contact David West
Runs treatment centres and counselling services for people suffering from alcohol, tranquilliser and drugs misuse. Organises

preventive education and training courses.
C B V P

ADFAM National

Unit 7, South Thames Studios, 5–11 Lavington Street, London SE1 0NZ
01–401 2079
Contact Anne Marshall
Sets up groups offering information, support and friendship to families of drug users; campaigns for improved treatment and services for drug users and their families. Runs information helpline.
C B V P

Association for Prevention of Addiction

5–7 Tavistock Place, London WC1H 9SS
01–383 5071
Contact Jean Rust
Advises and counsels drug users, their families and their friends. Provides information, training and educational materials.
C B V P

Hungerford Drug Project (Turning Point)

see under FAMILY WELFARE, p.18

RE-Solv – the Society for the Prevention of Solvent and Volatile Substance Abuse

St Mary's Chambers, 19 Station Road, Stone, Staffs ST15 8JP
0785–817885/46097
Aims to reduce and prevent solvent and volatile substance abuse; produces teaching materials for young people; provides information and advice.
C V P

TACADE (formerly Teachers' Advisory Council on Alcohol and Drug Education)

3rd Floor, Furness House, Trafford Park, Salford M5 2XJ
061–848 0351

Contact Sandra Jones
Provides training and support to teachers and health-care professionals. Can supply educational materials about alcohol and drug use and misuse, and information for young people and parents.
C P

Teen Challenge UK

Teen Challenge Centre, Penygroes Road, Gorslas, Llanelli, Dyfed
0269–842718
Contact John Macey
Offers practical and positive help to young people, especially those with problems, for example drug, solvent and alcohol abuse. Runs coffee houses and a residential centre.
C B V

Teetotallers Register

Jordans, 1c Grassington Road, Eastbourne, East Sussex BN20 7BP
Contact Wendy Whitehead
Offers support to anyone, adult or child, who wishes to abstain from alcohol. Arranges a number of recreational and educational activities; maintains a teetotallers register.
B V P

Turning Point

CAP House, 9/12 Long Lane, London EC1A 9HA
01–606 3947/9
Offers residential rehabilitation, counselling and information to people with alcohol or drug-related problems. Supports families and friends. Runs a variety of projects nationally, including telephone advice services.
C B V

UK Band of Hope Union

Hope House, 45 Great Peter Street, London SW1P 3LT
01–222 6809
Contact Christine Senior
Aims to encourage children and young

people to live healthy lives, free from drink and drugs problems. Provides educational materials, exhibitions, speakers etc.
C B V P

ALTERNATIVE THERAPY

Association for Dance Movement Therapy

99 South Hill Park, London NW3 2SP
Contact Lynn Crane
Aims to develop and promote dance movement therapy for the benefit of the general public.

British Association of Art Therapists

13c Northwood Road, Highgate, London N6 5TL
Contact G Hicks
Provides information (for a fee) on training courses for art therapists; maintains a register of practising art therapists.
B P

British Association for Dramatherapists

PO Box 98, Kirkbymoorside, York YO6 6EX
Contact Carol Taylor
A professional association. Able to provide information about dramatherapists working in your area.

British Herbal Medicine Association

PO Box 304, Bournemouth, Dorset BH7 6JZ
0202–433691
Aims to defend the right of the public to choose herbal remedies and to have free access to them; operates a code of practice for advertising herbal remedies; collects information on the safety and effectiveness of herbal medicines currently available.
P

British Holistic Medical Association

179 Gloucester Place, London NW1 6DX
01–262 5299
Contact Secretary
Aims to promote an awareness of the holistic approach to health. Runs courses and seminars to encourage self-healing; provides self-help tapes/books.
C B V

British Homoeopathic Association

27a Devonshire Street, London W1N 1RJ
01–935 2163
Contact General Secretary
Can provide a list of doctors practising homoeopathy.
C P

British Society for Music Therapy

69 Avondale Avenue, East Barnet, Herts EN4 8NB
01–368 8879
Contact Denize Christophers
Society aims to promote the use and development of music therapy in the treatment, education and rehabilitation of adults and children suffering from physical, mental or emotional handicap. May be able to provide information about music therapists in practice near you.
C B P

British Touch for Health Association

c/o Adrian Voce, 6 Railey Mews, London NW5 2PA
Can put enquirers in touch with local practitioners or groups.
B

Cancer Help Centre, Bristol

Grove House, Cornwallis Grove, Clifton, Bristol BS8 4PG
0272–743216
Contact Inquiry Desk
Offers a therapy programme working

at all levels of body, mind and spirit; provides a supportive link for cancer patients, their families and friends.
C B V P

Centre of Advice on Natural Alternatives

26 Lighthorne Road, Solihull, West Midlands B91 2BD
021–705 9961
Contact Catherine Barrett
Supplies information about natural alternatives to many modern processes.
P

Centre for Analytical Psychotherapy

College Hall, Malet Street, London WC1E 7HZ
01–625 6576
Contact Tom Ormay
Runs introductory course on psychotherapy; arranges individual and group psychotherapy (fee-paying).
P

Centre for Attitudinal Healing

PO Box 2023, London W12 9NY
Contact Hilde Heyman
Holds regular meetings (in groups) for meditation, relaxation, creative visualisations and discussions, to help people (not only parents) seek peace of mind and to develop a non-judgemental, loving attitude to themselves and other people.
C B V P

Children's Cancer Help Centre

PO Box 4, Orpington, Kent BR6 8Q7
0689–71587
Provides free advice, support, counselling and complementary therapies (relaxation, visualisation, meditation) to children with cancer or other life-threatening diseases.
C V P

Confederation of Healing Organisations

113 Hampstead Way, London NW11 7JN
01–455 2638
Contact Denis Haviland
A confederation of 750 healers in 15 healing associations throughout the UK. Aims to have healing accepted by the NHS and by the medical profession at large.
C B V P

National Federation of Spiritual Healers

Old Manor Farm Studio, Church Street, Sunbury on Thames, Middx TW7 6RG
0932–783164/5
Contact Audrey Murr Copland
Provides a national referral service for people seeking to make contact with a spiritual healer.
C B V P

New Approaches to Cancer

Addington Park, Maidstone, Kent ME19 5BL
0732–848336
Contact Joan Abbatt
Encourages the use of complementary methods of combating cancer, alongside more conventional techniques. Encourages the formation of self-help groups for patients and their families. Assists in the development of Cancer Help Centres throughout the UK.
C B V P

Society for Environmental Therapy

521 Foxhall Road, Ipswich, Suffolk IP3 8LW
Contact Hilary Davidson
Provides information on the environmental causes of disease; runs public enquiry service.
C

Stress Syndrome Foundation

Cedar House, Yalding, Kent
ME18 6JD
0622–814431
Contact Dr Audrey Livingstone-Booth
Aims to prevent stress-related and
stress-induced illnesses; runs training
courses for the public.
C V P

Topaz Line

BM Topaz, London WC1N 3XX
Contact Secretary
Offers a postal counselling service to
people who feel that their needs are
not adequately met by conventional
psychologies or therapeutic
frameworks.
P

Women's Natural Health Centre

1 Hillside, Highgate Road, London
NW5 1QT
01–482 3293
Contact Christianne Heal
Offers a variety of complementary
therapies to low-income women and
their children for low fees. Telephone
for appointments 9.30–12.30 am

FAMILY PLANNING

Association of Lawyers for the Defence of the Unborn

40 Bedford Street, London
WC2E 9EN
0202–426328
Contact Michael N M Bell
Campaigns to oppose abortion;
provides speakers for local groups.
P

British Pregnancy Advisory Service

Austy Manor, Wooten Wawen,
Solihull, West Midlands B95 6BX
05642–3225
Contact Diana Burt

Helps and advises women faced with
an unwanted pregnancy; also offers
pregnancy testing, contraception,
male and female sterilisation and help
with infertility.
C B P

Brook Advisory Centres

153a East Street, London SE17 2SD
01–708 1234/1390
Contact Alison Hadley
Runs 21 centres throughout the
country which offer confidential help
and advice to young people, including
information about contraception,
pregnancy tests, and counselling for a
wide range of sexual and emotional
difficulties.
C B P

Copper 7 Association

28 Finlay Gardens, Addlestone,
Weybridge, Surrey KT15 2XN
Contact Jeanette Morris
A contact group for women who have
suffered problems when using the
Copper 7 IUD. Campaigns to publicise
the risks to all users.
V P

Family Planning Association

Margaret Pyke House, 27–35
Mortimer Street, London W1N 7RJ
01–636 7866
Contact Charlotte Owen
Runs National Family Planning
Information Service, giving details of
free NHS family planning services;
maintains a resource centre and
personal information service on all
aspects of birth control, and a book
centre with mail order section.
C B V P

Foresight – the Association for the Promotion of Conceptual Care

The Old Vicarage, Church Lane,
Witley, Godalming, Surrey GU8 5PN
0428–794500
Contact Belinda Barnes

Promotes optimum health in both parents prior to the conception of a child, with a view to minimising the chances of infertility, miscarriage and/ or handicap or compromised health in the baby.
C B V P

International Planned Parenthood Federation

Regent's College, Regent's Park, London NW1 4NS
01–486 0741
Contact Sunetra Puri
A federation of independent family planning associations in 125 countries. Produces a wide range of publications on family planning topics.
C B P

LIFE (Save the Unborn Child)

118–120 Warwick Street, Leamington Spa, Warks CV32 4QY
0926–21587/311667
Contact N Scarisbrick
Aims to help women avoid abortion by offering free pregnancy counselling, accommodation and help to any pregnant woman.
B V P

National Abortion Campaign

Wesley House, 4 Wild Court, London WC2B 5AU
Contact Leonora Lloyd
Campaigning group which seeks to secure for women the right to make their own decision about abortion, and to provide adequate abortion facilities within the NHS. Also concerned to improve sex education and to make it easier for all women to get help and information about contraception.
B V P

National Association for the Childless

318 Summer Lane, Birmingham, B19 3RL
021–359 4887

Contact David J Owens
Offers advice, support and information to people with infertility problems.
C B V P

National Association of Natural Family Planning Teachers

NFP Centre, Birmingham Maternity Hospital, Queen Elizabeth Medical Centre, Edgbaston, Birmingham B15 2TG
021–472 1377 ext 4219; secretary **051–526 7663**
Contact Wyn Worthington
Offers a clinic and domicilary service to parents wishing to use natural methods of family planning, and training for medicine and non-medical people who wish to become teachers of natural family planning.
C B V P

Pregnancy Advisory Service

13 Charlotte Street, London W1P 1HD
01–637 8999
Contact Tara Kaufman
Provides advice and help to women with unwanted pregnancies and treatment for those with lawful grounds for termination. Promotes education and research on pregnancy, contraception and abortion. Also smear tests, post-abortion counselling, post-coital birth control and artificial insemination by donor.

Society for the Protection of Unborn Children

7 Tufton Street, London SW1P 3QN
01–222 5845
Contact John Smeaton
Campaigns for the repeal of the 1967 Abortion Act and for positive alternatives which respect the right to life.
B V P

Women's Health and Reproductive Rights Information Centre

52–54 Featherstone Street, London
EC1Y 8RT
01–251 6332/6580
An independent information and
resource centre for all issues covering
women's health, including infertility.
C P

MATERNITY SERVICES AND BABIES

Association of Breastfeeding Mothers

10 Herschell Road, London SE23 1EG
01–778 4769
Contact Elizabeth Dudley
Holds support group meetings for
mothers throughout the country; runs
a telephone counselling service;
provides information and advice.
C B V P

Association for Improvements in the Maternity Services

163 Liverpool Road, London N1 0RF
01–278 5628
Contact Christine Rodgers
Offers information, support and
advice to parents on all aspects of
maternity care, including parents'
rights, the choices available, technical
interventions, natural childbirth, and
complaints procedures.
B V P

Association of Radical Midwives

62 Greetby Hill, Ormskirk, Lancs
L39 2DT
0695–72776
Contact Ishbel Kargar
Works to improve maternity services,
especially within the NHS; campaigns
to preserve and enhance choices in
childbirth for all women and to re-
establish the full role of midwives.
B P

Baby Life Support Systems (BLISS)

44/45 Museum Street, London
WC1A 1LY
01–831 9393
Contact Co-ordinator
Raises money for special equipment
to care for new-born babies in
hospital, and to pay for training
courses for medical and nursing staff.
Runs Bliss-Link, a support service for
parents of babies in intensive care.
C B V P

Birthright (National Fund for Childbirth Research)

27 Sussex Place, Regent's Park,
London NW1 4SP
01–723 9296/01–262 5337
Contact Vivienne Parry
Funds medical research for the better
health of women and babies;
encourages research and new
treatments for a wide range of
gynaecological and obstetric
problems, especially those
encountered before, during and after
birth.
C B V

Cervical Stitch Network

15 Matcham Road, London E11 3LE
Contact Ros Kane
Provides information, support, advice
and contacts for women who need, or
might need, a cervical stitch in
pregnancy.
C P V

Foundation for the Study of Infant Deaths (Cot Death Research & Support)

15 Belgrave Square, London
SW1X 8PS
01–235 0965/01–235 1721
(answerphone)
Contact June Reed/Catherine York
Offers support and counselling to
bereaved parents; promotes research
into the causes and prevention of
sudden and unexpected infant deaths

('cot deaths'); gives advice and information.
C B V P

International Centre for Active Birth

55 Dartmouth Park Road, London NW5 1SL
01–267 3006
Contact Keith Brainin/Janet Balaskas
Offers classes to pregnant women and their partners to prepare for a natural, active birth. Active teachers training course, post-natal exercise and baby and toddler programme. Water birth pools are available for hire for use in home and in hospitals.
B V P

La Leche League of Great Britain

PO Box BM 3424, London WC1N 3XX
01–242 1278/01–405 5011
Contact Esther E Culpin
Provides information and support, primarily through personal help, to women who wish to breastfeed their babies. Runs a 24-hour counselling service.
C B V P

Maternity Alliance

15 Britannia Street, London WC1X 9JP
01–837 1265
Contact Lyn Durward
Campaigns for improvements in health care, social and financial support for parents-to-be and for mothers, fathers and babies in the first year of life, and for improvements in the legal rights of parents during and after pregnancy. Runs an information service.
P

Maternity Links

The Old Co-op, 42 Chelsea Road, Easton, Bristol BS5 6AF
0272–541487/558495
Contact Shaheen Chaudhry

Maintains a team of linkworkers to act as advocates, befrienders, and passers-on of information to non-English-speaking mothers who have difficulty in receiving maternity care from the NHS. Home tutors (volunteers) are available to teach these mothers English should they desire it.

Miscarriage Association

see under FAMILY WELFARE, p.40

National Association for Maternal and Child Welfare

1 South Audley Street, London W1Y 6JS
01–491 1315
Contact Maxine Offredy
Runs a consultancy and advisory service for people concerned with promoting maternal and child welfare. Organises courses in parent education, child care and human development.
C V P

National Campaign for Nursery Education

23 Albert Street, London NW1 7LU
Contact V Kotzen
Campaigns for increased play and education facilities for children under 5 as promised under the 1944 Education Act.
B V

National Childbirth Trust

Alexandra House, Oldham Terrace, Acton, London W3 6NH
01–992 8637
Contact Hanna Corbishley
Promotes education for parenthood; campaigns for flexibility and choice in birth arrangements; supports breastfeeding where possible. Runs antenatal classes, breastfeeding counselling and postnatal support branches.
C B V P

National Information for Parents of Prematures: Education, Resources and Support (NIPPERS)

c/o The Sam Segal Perinatal Unit, St Mary's Hospital, Praed Street, London W2 1NY
Contact Caroline Kerr-Smith, 49 Allison Road, London W3
01–992 9301
Encourages the setting up of support groups; helps parents to make contact with other parents of prematures; provides information.
C B V P

Pre-Eclamptic Toxaemia Society
see p.85

Society to Support Home Confinements

Lydgate, Lydgate Lane, Wolsingham, Bishop Auckland, Co Durham DL13 3HA
09565–528044
Contact Margaret Whyte
Offers support, advice and assistance to women who want a home confinement but who meet with difficulties in arranging midwifery attendance.
B V

MENTAL HEALTH

Association for Post-Natal Illness

7 Gowan Avenue, London SW6 6RH
01–731 4867
Contact Sheila Hamblett
Advises and supports women suffering from post-natal depression. Maintains a network of volunteers to support sufferers.

Federation of Phobic Care Organisations

Greater London House, 547/551 High Road, Leytonstone, London E11 4PR
01–558 6012
Co-ordinates the activities of all organisations in the field of phobic care; promotes the interests of adults and children with phobias. Can provide information about phobic care organisations to parents.
C B V P

Fellowship of Depressives Anonymous

36 Chestnut Avenue, Beverley, North Humberside HU17 9QU
0482–860619
Contact Pat Freya
Supports and encourages people suffering from, or who have suffered from, depression, on a mutual help basis; provides information; promotes the formation of local groups.
C B P

Jewish Welfare Board

Stuart Young House, 221 Golders Green Road, London NW11 9DN
01–485 3282 ext 265
Contact Social Work Department
Offers help to the families of mentally-ill people.
C B V

Manic Depression Fellowship IYQ

51 Sheen Road, Richmond, Surrey TW9
01–332 1087 (messages only)
Helps sufferers from manic depression and their relatives; runs local self-help groups; supplies information.
C B V P

National Schizophrenia Fellowship
see under FAMILY WELFARE, p.18

Richmond Fellowship for Community Mental Health

8 Addison Road, London W14 8DL
01–603 6373/4/5
Contact Family Worker
Provides residential accommodation, therapeutic communities and workshops for rehabilitation for

people who are or who have been emotionally or mentally disturbed, or who are at risk, or who are overcoming a problem involving drug or alcohol abuse.
C B V

Schizophrenia, a National Emergency

5th Floor, 120 Regent Street, London W1A 5FE
01–434 0150/734 2471/494 4840
Contact Linda Snell
Supports schizophrenia sufferers and their families.
C V P

Schizophrenia Association of Great Britain

Bryn Hyrfyd, The Crescent, Bangor, Gwynedd LL57 2AG
0248–354048
Contact Gretel Leeb
Helps psychiatric patients and their relatives; runs telephone and postal advice service.
C V P

Tavistock Institute of Medical Psychology

Tavistock Centre, Belsize Lane, London NW3 5BA
01–435 7111
Contact Information Office
Promotes the study and practice of psychotherapy; runs Tavistock Institute of Marital Studies and Career and Educational Counselling service.
C P

SPECIFIC CONDITIONS

AAA (Action Against Allergy)

43 The Downs, London SW20 8HG
01–947 5082
Contact Amelia Nathan Hill
Provides information to allergy sufferers; works for recognition and for improved treatment facilities for allergy-related illness.
C V P

Aid for Children with Tracheotomies

Station House, Market Bosworth, Nuneaton, Warks CV13 0PE
0455–290718
Contact S P Davies
Raises funds to purchase medical equipment; supports and gives practical advice to parents; establishes local self-help groups.
C B P

AIDS Care, Education and Training (ACET)

PO Box 1323, London W5 5TF
01–840 7879
A new church-based AIDS charity. Volunteers are trained to provide a national network of practical home care backed by a system of grants, nursing staff and 24-hour on-call service. ACET is also committed to education in schools.

Amnesia Association

St Charles Hospital, Exmoor Street, London W10 6DZ
Contact Secretary
Offers help and advice to patients with amnesia and their carers.
C B V P

Anglemann Syndrome Support Group

15 Palace Crescent, Waterlooville, Portsmouth, Hants POY 5UR
0705–264224
Contact Sheila Woolven
Aims to further a better understanding of Anglemann Syndrome among parents and professionals and to provide support and assistance to parents of children with this condition.

Anorexia and Bulimia Nervosa Association

Tottenham Women's Health Centre, Annexe C, Tottenham Town Hall, London N5 4RX
01–885 3936

Contact Viv Walkerdine
Provides confidential help and support to women and girls with eating problems. Runs a helpline; maintains a national network of self-help groups.
C V P

Apert Syndrome Support Group

Fullers Barn, 9 The Green, Loughton, Milton Keynes, Bucks MK5 8AW
0908 608557
Contact P Walker
Provides information, contact and emotional support to patients with this condition.
P

Arthritis Care

6 Grosvenor Crescent, London SW1X 7ER
01–235 0902
Contact Information Officer
Works to further the well-being of all people who have rheumatism and arthritis, and to improve their quality of life. The 35 group helps young people and their parents. Runs specially-adapted holiday homes and self-catering units.
C B V P

Arthrogryposis Group

1 The Oaks, Common Mead Lane, Gillingham, Dorset SP8 4SW
Contact Diana Piercy
Maintains a network of contacts among arthrogrypotics and their families; aims to assist parents to help their children to reach their fullest potential. Raises money for research.
C B V P

Association to Combat Huntington's Chorea

34a Station Road, Hinckley, Leics LE10 1AP
0455–615558
Maintains a network of local self-help groups, and a national social work and counselling service. Promotes

research, publicises and alleviates the plight of affected families.
C B V P

Association for the Education and Welfare of the Visually Handicapped

4 Stockdale Place, Westfield Road, Edgbaston, Birmingham B15 3XH
021–454 7053
Contact J M Stone
Holds regional meetings, day and weekend conferences; runs regional groups. Members include teachers, social workers; parents welcome to join.
C B V P

Association of Glycogen Storage Diseases (UK)

9 Lindop Road, Hale, Altrincham, Cheshire WA15 9DZ
Contact Ann Phillips
Runs a contact and support group for all people affected by some form of Glycogen Storage Disease; acts as a focus for educational, scientific and charitable activities related to this disorder.

Association for Research into Restricted Growth

103 St Thomas Avenue, West Town, Hayling Island, Hants PO11 0EU
0705–461742/0923–770759
Contact Tina Webb
Provides information, help, advice, encouragement and opportunities for social contact to persons of restricted growth and their families.
C B V P

Asthma Society and Friends of the Asthma Research Council

300 Upper Street, London N1 2XX
01–226 2260
Contact Monica Robb
Gives help and advice to people with asthma so that they may live healthier and more active lives. Promotes

research into the causes, treatment and cure of asthma.
C B V P

Behcets Syndrome Society

3 Belgrave Street, Haxby Road, York YO3 7YY
0904–637310
Contact J A Buckle
Provides information and advice; runs 24-hour helpline. May be able to offer grant aid if all other sources fail.
C V P

Body Positive

PO Box 493, London W14 0TF
01–373 9124 (helpline)/**01–835 1045** (office)
A self-help group of people concerned with HIV and AIDS; most members of the group are HIV antibody positive. Runs a telephone helpline, visits hospitals, offers counselling, maintains advice and support groups.
C B V P

British Association of Cancer United Patients (BACUP)

121/123 Charterhouse Street, London EC1M 6AA
01–608 1661
Contact Cancer Information Service
Provides a free, confidential cancer information service throughout the UK by telephone and letter; produces advice and information booklets; runs a counselling service (at present, for London only) for patients and their families.
C V P

British Colostomy Association

38–39 Eccleston Square, London SW1V 1PB
01–828 5175
Offers information, advice and support to colostomy patients and their families.
C B V

British Diabetic Association

10 Queen Anne Street, London W1M 0BD
01–323 1531
Contact Hazel Bristow
Promotes research into the causes and treatment of diabetes; provides information; maintains a network of local branches; organises educational and recreational activities for diabetics of all ages; raises money for research.
C B V P

British Digestive Foundation

3 St Andrew's Place, London NW1 4LB
Produces information and advice leaflets on many gastro-intestinal diseases, to help sufferers and their families; raises money for research.
C B V P

British Epilepsy Association

Anstey House, 40 Hanover Square, Leeds LS3 1BE
0532–439393
Contact R Pugh
Provides advice, information and support for people with epilepsy and their families; organises national network of self-help groups.
C B V P

British Kidney Patient Federation

Bordon, Hampshire, GU35 9JP
04203–2021/2
Contact E D Ward
Runs three holiday dialysis centres; gives financial support and advice to patients and their relatives; campaigns for improved NHS facilities and to raise funds.
C B V P

British Lung Foundation

12A Onslow Gardens, London SW7 3AP
01–581 0226
Provides advice and information to people who suffer from diseases of

the chest and lungs.
C B V P

British Migraine Association

178a High Road, Byfleet, Surrey
KT14 7ED
09323–52468
Contact Jo Liddell
Offers information about research in
progress and the latest treatments
available to migraine sufferers;
supports research.
C V P

British Organ Donor Society (BODY)

Balsham, Cambridge, CB1 6DL
0223–893636
Contact Pauline Atkinson
BODY is a self-help and support group
for donor, recipient and waiting
recipient families.
C V P

British Retinitis Pigmentosa Society

Greens Norton Court, Greens Norton,
Towcester, Northants NN12 8BS
0372–53276
Contact Lynda Drummond-Walker
Offers counselling, support and
encouragement to all those suffering
from this disorder; encourages the
formation of local self-help and
support groups; supports medical
research.
C B V P

British SLE Aid Group (Lupus Group)

25 Linden Crescent, Woodford Green,
Essex 1G8 0DG
01–235 0902 (via Arthritis Care)
Contact Cheryl Marcus
Organises fundraising events to
sponsor research and to purchase
necessary medical equipment and
care for patients. Provides information
for patients and their families.
C B V P

British Tinnitus Association/RNID Tinnitus Support Services

105 Gower Street, London
WC1E 6AH
01–387 4803/436 7637
Contact David Wiggins
Helps sufferers maintain contact with
each other; raises funds; campaigns
for greater public recognition of the
problem.
C B V P

Brittle Bone Society

Unit 4, Block 20, Carlunie Road,
Dunsinane Estate, Dundee DD2 3QT
0382–817771
Provides financial aid, advice and
information to patients and their
families, and raises funds to support
research.
C B V P

Cancer Aftercare and Rehabilitation Society

21 Zetland Road, Bristol, Avon
BS6 7AH
0272–427419
Maintains 50 support groups to
provide emotional and practical
support for cancer patients, their
relatives and friends. Runs an
information service and phonelink
scheme.
C B V

Cancer and Leukaemia in Childhood Trust

11/12 Fremantle Square, Cotham,
Bristol BS6 5TI
0272–248844
Contact Gill Whiteside
Supports affected children and their
families; helps provide the best
possible care and treatment;
promotes research. Provides
accommodation for families of
children undergoing treatment at
hospitals in the South West region. A
team of CLIC domiciliary care nurses
also covers this area.
C B V P

Cancer Link

17 Britannia Street, London
WC1X 9JN
01–833 2451
Provides support and information to
people with cancer, their families and
friends. Acts as resource to cancer
support and self help groups
throughout Britain, and helps people
set up new ones.
C V P

Cancer Relief Macmillan Fund

Anchor House, 15/19 Britten Street,
London SW3 3TZ
01–351 7811
Contact Susan Butler
Provides skilled care and support for
all cancer patients at every stage of
their illness. Funds teams of specially
trained nurses to care for patients in
their homes and builds specialist
cancer care units and day-care
facilities. Can make grants to cancer
patients in financial difficulties.
C B V P

Charcot-Marrie-Tooth International (UK)

c/o 121 Lavernock Road, Penarth,
Wales CF6 2QG
0222–709537
Contact Margaret Reed
Offers support and assistance to
people who suffer from CMT disease,
and to those who care for them.
Promotes research into treatment and
prevention.
C B P

Chest, Heart and Stroke Association Volunteer Stroke Scheme

c/o Manor Farm, Appleton, Abingdon,
Oxon OX13 4JR
0865–862954
Organises local volunteers to help
stroke patients re-learn basic skills.
C B V P

Child Growth Foundation

2 Mayfield Avenue, London W4 1PW
01–995 0275/994–7625
Raises funds to support research into
the causes and cures of growth
disorders in children; offers
counselling to families where children
have these disorders.
C B V P

Coeliac Society

PO Box 220, High Wycombe, Bucks
HP11 2HY
Contact J Austin
Promotes the welfare of all children
and adults who are medically-
diagnosed coeliacs, and those with
dermatitis herpetiformis.
C B V P

Community Cancer Care

15 Phillips Road, Barham, Ipswich,
Suffolk 1P6 0AZ
0473–830774
Offers aid, support and comfort to
families whose lives have been
affected by cancer; promotes self-
help through shared experience and
support; runs an information bureau;
maintains caravan holiday facilities for
cancer families.
C B P

Crohn's in Childhood Research Appeal

Parkgate House, 356 West Barnes
Lane, Motspur Park, Surrey KT3 6NB
01–949 6209
Contact Margaret Lee
Establishes self-help groups for
patients and their families; raises
funds to further research; campaigns
for greater awareness of the disease.
C B P

Cystic Fibrosis Research Trust

Alexandra House, 5 Blyth Road,
Bromley, Kent
01–464 7211
Contact Sandra Kennedy

Helps and advises parents with children suffering from cystic fibrosis; educates the public about the disease; finances research and helps promote diagnosis in young children.
C B V P

Cystic Hygroma and Haemangioma Support Group
Villa Fontane, Church Road, Worth, Crawley, West Sussex RH10 4RS
0293–885901/883901
Contact David Poulter
Provides information, contact and support for families and sufferers; aims to set up local self-help groups; raises funds for research.
V P

Dyspraxia Trust
13 Old Hale Way, Hitchin, Herts SG5 1XJ
0462–54986
Contact Stella White
Aims to put parents and children in touch with other sufferers, locally and nationally, and to encourage a wider understanding of the condition.

Dystonia Society
Omnibus Workspace, 39–41 North Road, London N7 9DP
01–700 4594
Contact Michael Eaton
Offers support and advice to people suffering from a range of neurological conditions including generalised dystonia, blepharospasm, torticollis and writer's cramp. Runs a telephone helpline; sets up local groups for sufferers.
C B V P

Dystrophic Epidermolysis Bullosa Research Association
Suite 4, 1st Floor, 1 King's Road, Crowthorne, Berks RG11 7BG
0344–771961
Gives support and friendship to patients and their families; runs a contact service and various welfare services. Provides information, promotes research.
C B V P

Eating Disorders Association
(formerly Anorexic Aid, and Anorexic Family Aid and National Information Centre)
Sackville Place, 44/48 Magdalen Street, Norwich, Norfolk NR3 1JE
0603–621414
Offers help, support and understanding to anyone suffering from anorexia or bulimia nervosa, their families and friends. Maintains a nationwide advice and information service.
For advice about education and local self-help groups contact The Priory Centre, 11 Priory Road, High Wycombe, Bucks HP13 6SL, Tel. 0494–21431.
C B V P

Ehlers Danlose Syndrome Support Group
2 High Garth, Richmond, North Yorkshire DL10 4DG
Contact Valerie Burrows
Links sufferers and parents of sufferers for mutual encouragement and support. Publishes advice leaflets.
P

Elimination of Leukaemia Fund
5 Camberwell Church Street, London SE5 8TR
01–703 7038
Contact Martyn Hall
Provides information and advice to parents with a leukaemia sufferer in the family.
C V P

Endometriosis Society
65 Holmdene Avenue, Herne Hill, London SE24 9LD
01–737 4764
Encourages self-help and mutual

support among women with this condition; offers information, help and advice; promotes research into infertility.
C B V P

Family Heart Association

PO Box 116, Kidlington, Oxford OX5 1DT
08675–79125
Offers support to people suffering from familial hyperlipidaemias, and encourages further research into the condition. Provides information on self-help and diets.
C B V P

Food and Chemical Allergy Association

27 Ferringham Lane, Ferring-by-Sea, West Sussex BN1 5NB
0903–41178
Contact Ellen Mary Rothera
Helps anyone who suffers from allergy-based illness: supplies (for a fee) information and practical advice.
V P

Friedreich's Ataxia Group

The Common, Cranleigh, Surrey GU6 8SB
0483–272741
Contact Sue Grice
Gives advice and assistance to sufferers and their families, and helps raise money for research.
C B V P

Guillain Barre Syndrome Support Group

Foxley, Holdingham, Sleaford, Lincs NG34 8NR
0529–304615
Contact Glennys Saiders
Provides emotional and practical support to patients, their families and friends; raises funds; establishes local groups.
C B V P

Haemophilia Society

123 Westminster Bridge Road, London SE1 7HR
01–928 2020
Contact David G Watters
Gives advice, information, help and financial support to people suffering from haemophilia. Maintains network of local groups.
C B V P

Hairline International

Hill Vellacott, Post and Mail House, Colmore Circus, Birmingham B4 6AT
Contact Ruth Brown
An international support network for patients (including children) who have lost, or who are losing, their hair through alopecia. Offers telephone counselling, news about treatments, general information. Can put patients in touch with other sufferers.
B V P

Headway – National Head Injuries Association

200 Mansfield Road, Nottingham, NG1 3HX
0602–622382
Sets up self-help and support groups for patients with head injuries and for their relatives facing problems created by these. Provides information on how to cope with patients' problems, and offers help to families. Raises funds for day-care, residential and assessment centres.
C B V P

Heart to Heart

PO Box 7, High Street, Pershore, Worcs
A self-help group which gives practical advice and support to people who are about to undergo heart surgery.
V

Heart Line Association

5 Russet Gardens, Camberley, Surrey
GU15 2LG
0276–61824
Contact Eileen Clark
Provides an informal forum for
parents of children with heart
complaints. Maintains local self-help
groups concerned with children's
home environment, education and
future employment.
C B V P

Herpes Association

41 North Road, London N7 9DP
01–609 9061
Contact Marian Nichols
Offers help and advice to people with
herpes simplex. Runs a telephone
helpline; offers counselling; co-
ordinates local self-help groups.
C B V P

Hyperthyroidism Self-Help

47 Crawford Avenue, Tyldesley,
Manchester M29 8ET
0942–874740
Contact Caroline Worthington
Offers reassurance by letter and
telephone for people with a
hyperthyroid condition.

Hysterectomy Support Group

11 Henryson Road, London SE4 1HL
01–690 5987
Contact Sue Mack
Encourages self-help through the
informal sharing of experiences and
by providing information about
hysterectomy. Provides support to
women and their partners.
Encourages the setting up of new
support groups.
B V P

Ileostomy Association of Great Britain and Ireland

Amblehurst House, Black Scotch
Lane, Mansfield, Notts NG18 4PF
Helps people with ileostomies back to
a full life; works to improve ileostomy
management techniques; provides
information; maintains network of
local branches.
C B V P

Infantile Hypercalcaemia Foundation Ltd (incorporating Williams Syndrome)

Mulberry Cottage, 37 Mulberry Green,
Old Harlow, Essex CM17 0EY
0279–27214
Contact Lady Cooper
Holds meetings for parents, children,
doctors and other interested parties.
Gives information and advice to
parents. Raises funds for research.
Funds holidays for families.
C B V P

International Glaucoma Association

c/o King's College Hospital, Denmark
Hill, London SE5 9RS
01–274 6222 ext 2934 (Mon and
Thurs only)
Provides support for people suffering
from glaucoma and those concerned
with its diagnosis and treatment.
Offers useful information to patients
and the general public. Supports
research.
C P V

Leukaemia Care Society

PO Box 82, Exeter, Devon EX2 5DP
0392–218514
Contact Fred W Connett
Provides information, support,
financial help and holidays to people
suffering from leukaemia and/or allied
blood disorders, and their families.
C B V P

Leukaemia Research Fund

43 Great Ormond Street, London
WC1N 3JJ
01–405 0101
Contact Douglas L Osborne

Largely a fund-raising charity; produces patient information booklets.

C B V P

LINK – the Neurofibromatosis Association

D15, London House, 26–40 Kensington High Street, London W8 9PF

01–983 2222 ext 2226

Contact Clare Peperell

A mutual support group for people suffering from neurofibromatosis and their families, providing advice, counselling and information.

London Lighthouse

111–117 Lancaster Road, London W11 1QT

01–792 1200

Contact Caspar Thomson

Acts as a residential and support centre for people affected by AIDS. Offers a social/drop-in centre; counselling, health, education and training programmes; domicilary support; convalescent, respite and terminal care.

C V

Lupus Group, Arthritis Care

6 Grosvenor Crescent, London SW1X 7ER

01–235 0902

Contact E Brain

Provides communication between sufferers; arranges educational and recreational meetings; can provide financial assistance and advice.

C B P

Malcolm Sargeant Cancer Fund for Children

14 Abingdon Road, London W8 6AF

01–937 4548

Contact Sylvia Darley

For the welfare of all young people (under 21) who have any form of cancer.

Marfan Association

70 Greenways, Courtmoor, Fleet, Hants GU13 9XD

0252–617320/617908

Contact Diane Rust

Aims to support patients and to enable them to make contact with one another and with appropriate medical care. Offers advice and information. Supports research. Holds annual Marfan Information Day.

C B V P

Marie Curie Cancer Care

28 Belgrave Square, London SW1X 8QG

01–235 3325

Contact Claire Batchelor

Cares for cancer patients and their families through residential Marie Curie Homes and a nationwide Marie Curie Community Nursing Service, which is free of charge to the patient. Also involved in cancer research and education.

C B V P

Michael McGough Foundation Against Liver Disease in Children

PO Box 494, Western Avenue, London W3 0SH

01–992 3400 ext 6131

Provides emotional support, information and advice to families; raises funds to support research and treatment.

C B V P

Microcephaly Support Group

17 Tennyson Rise, East Grinstead, West Sussex RH19 1SQ

0342–28066

Contact Jill Booker

Promotes contact and mutual support between parents of microcephalic children, and encourages problem-sharing and befriending.

Migraine Trust

45 Great Ormond Street, London
WC1N 3HD
01–278 2676
Contact Director
Provides information, advice and
counselling to migraine sufferers and
their families; encourages self-help
groups; raises funds for research, and
supports the Princess Margaret
Children's Migraine Clinic at Charing
Cross Hospital, London.
C B V P

Motor Neurone Disease Association

61 Derngate, Northampton NN1 1UE
0604–22269/250505
Contact Tricia Holmes
Provides care for patients and
supports medical research.
C B V P

Multiple Sclerosis Society of Great Britain and Northern Ireland

25 Effie Road, Fulham, London
SW6 1EE
01–736 6267
Provides a welfare and support
service through a network of 350
branches and associations. Runs
holiday and short-stay homes. Funds
research.
C B V P

Muscular Dystrophy Group of Great Britain and Northern Ireland

Nattrass House, 35 Macaulay Road,
London SW4 0QP
01–720 8055
Contact Fran Wilson
Assists sufferers, maintains local
contact and support groups, raises
money for research. Provides advice
and information.
C B V P

Myalgic Encephalomyelitis (ME) Association

PO Box 8, Stanford-le-Hope, Essex
SS17 8EX
0375–642466
Contact Peter Blackman
Raises funds to sponsor research and
to help support sufferers. Maintains
local groups, runs a telephone
helpline.
C B V P

Myotonic Dystrophy Support Group

c/o 175 Carlton Hill, Carlton, Notts
0602–871646
Contact Margaret Bowler
Provides information and support to
sufferers and carers.
V P

Naevus Support Group

58 Necton Road, Wheathamstead,
St Albans, Herts AL4 8AU
058283–2853
Contact John and Renate O'Neill
Provides information about birthmarks
and puts parents of children with
birthmarks in touch with each other.
V P

Narcolepsy Association (United Kingdom)

6 Derwent Close, Holme Chapel,
Crewe, CW4 7JY
Contact Dorothy Pownall
Promotes the interests of people with
this illness, encourages research,
provides advice, support and a
meeting place for fellow-sufferers.
C P

National Aids Trust

Room 1402, Euston Tower, 296
Euston Road, London NW1 3DN
01–388 1188 ext 3200
An umbrella body, designed to
promote and co-ordinate voluntary
sector effort in the field of AIDS and
HIV infection. May be able to provide

information about local voluntary AIDS care initiatives.

National Ankylosing Spondylitis Society

6 Grosvenor Crescent, London SW1X 7ER
Contact Fergus J Rogers
Maintains local groups; runs an advice and information service for sufferers; encourages research.
C B P

National Association for Colitis and Crohn's Disease

98a London Road, St Albans, Herts AL1 1NX
0727–44296 (answerphone)
Contact Leslie Parrott
Provides information and contact for sufferers, their relatives and friends. Promotes research, and raises funds. Maintains network of area groups.
C B V P

National Association of Laryngectomee Clubs

4th Floor, 39 Eccleston Square, London SW1V 1PB
01–834 2857
Contact L Abrams
Encourages the formation of clubs for laryngectomees, and works to promote their welfare.
C B V

National Association for the Relief of Paget's Disease

413 Middleton Road, Middleton, Manchester M24 4QZ
021–643 1998
Contact A Stansfield
Promotes research and raises funds; provides information to sufferers and their relatives.

National Centre for Epilepsy

Chalfont Centre, Chalfont St Peter, Gerrards Cross, Bucks SL9 0RJ
02407–3991

Provides assessment, rehabilitation, training and long-term care to people with epilepsy; promotes research; runs an advice and information service. There is also an assessment unit for people with mental handicap and epilepsy.
C V P

National Diabetes Foundation

177a Tennison Road, London SE25 5NF
01–656 5467
Contact Arthur Bennett
Raises funds; gives non-medical advice; maintains a panel of doctors to give general help and advice to parents of diabetic children.
C B V P

National Eczema Society

Tavistock House North, Tavistock Square, London WC1H 9SR
01–388 4097
Contact John Randall
Aims to improve the quality of life for eczema sufferers and their families. Maintains network of local branches; arranges social and educational meetings; provides information.
B V P

National Federation of Kidney Patients' Associations

Acorn Lodge, Woodsets, Nr Worksop, Notts S81 8AT
Contact Margaret Jackson
Promotes the welfare of people suffering from kidney disease or renal failure. Campaigns for improved treatment and facilities; encourages self-help among patients, and provides advice and information; supports a network of local associations; helps to provide equipment, holidays and other practical help for patients and their families.
C B V P

National Meningitis Trust

Fern House, Bath Road, Stroud,
Gloucester GL5 3TJ
04536–71738
Supports patients with meningitis and
their families; raises funds; provides
advice and information.
C B V P

National Reye's Syndrome Foundation of the UK

15 Nicholas Gardens, Pyrford,
Woking, Surrey GU22 8SD
09323–46843
Supports families of patients who
have suffered from Reye's
Syndrome; raises funds to sponsor
research.
C V P

National Society for Children with Intestinal Disorders

39 The Ridings, Thorley Park, Bishops
Stortford, Herts CM23 4EH
0279–505482
Contact Allison Hutchinson
Offers support to sick children and
their parents; funds research and
purchases equipment.
C V P

Neuroblastoma Society

Woodlands, Ordsall Park Road,
Retford, Notts DN22 7PJ
0777–709238
Contact N W S Oldridge
Raises funds for research; publishes
an information booklet for parents.
C B V P

Noonan's Syndrome Society

27 Pinfold Lane, Cheslyn Hay,
Nr Walsall, Staffs WS6 7HP
0922–416417
Contact Sheila Brown
Provides support and information for
families with a member who has
Noonan's Syndrome; arranges
contacts between parents.
Offers support and information.

Arranges get-togethers around the
country. Has medical advisers.
C B V P

Organic Acidaemias UK

5 Saxon Road, Ashford, Middx
TW15 1QL
0784–245989
Contact David Priddy
Acts as a contact point for parents of
children with these protein related
disorders; provides information,
including advice on diets.
P

Organisation for Sickle Cell Anaemia Research (OSCAR)

22 Pellat Grove, Wood Green, London
N22 5PL
01–889 3300/4844
Contact Laris Fisher
Gives information, counselling,
support and advice to people with this
disorder, and to their families; raises
funds for research; works to increase
public awareness.
C B V P

Overeaters Anonymous

PO Box 19, Stretford, Manchester
M32 9EB
Contact Public Information Officer
Maintains a network of people who,
through shared experience and
mutual support, are recovering from
overeating. Holds group meetings and
workshops.
B P

Perthes Association

49 Great Stone Road, Northfield,
Birmingham B31 2LR
021–477 4515
Contact Gill Draper
Provides advice and comfort to
parents of childen suffering from
Perthes Disease; offers practical help

and puts them in touch with others in the same situation in the same locality.

C B V P

Phobic Action

Greater London House, 547/551 High Road, Leytonstone, London E11 4PR
01–558 3463/6012
Contact Jeff Fendall
Develops, supports and maintains self-help groups for people suffering from phobias and extreme anxiety.

C B V P

Prader-Willi Syndrome Association (UK)

30 Follet Drive, Abbots Langley, Herts WD5 0LP
0923–67543
Contact Rosemary Erskine
Makes contact with, and supports, families with sufferers from this disorder; provides information; raises funds to sponsor research.

C B P

Pre-Eclamptic Toxaemia Society

Ty Iago, High Street, Llanberis, Caernarvon, Gwynedd LL55 4HB
0286–872477
Contact Dawn James
A self-help and support group for women who have suffered from pre-eclampsia, or who are suffering from this condition now. Provides information and encourages research into prevention and cure.

C B V P

Psoriasis Association

7 Milton Street, Northampton NN2 7JG
0604–711129
Contact Linda Henley
Encourages the formation of local self-help groups for sufferers; gives information and advice; raises funds to sponsor research.

C B V P

Renal Society

41 Mutton Place, London NW1 8DF
01–485 9775
Contact Grace Blick
Gives encouragement to renal patients, especially those whose treatment is by diet alone and who probably do not belong to a renal unit.

C

Research Trust for Metabolic Diseases in Children

53 Beam Street, Nantwich, Cheshire CW5 5NF
0270–629782
Contact Lesley Greene
Works to further medical research into metabolic diseases in children; raises funds; makes grants to help affected children; arranges meetings for contact and mutual support between families.

C B V P

Sanfilippo Letter Magazine

The Gables, Rock Lane, Standen, Stafford ST21 6QZ
0782–70487
Contact Linda Matthews
Provides personal contact for parents of Sanfilippo children by means of letter-writing groups.

Sarcoidosis Association UK

19 Ashurst Close, St Helens, Merseyside WA11 9DN
0744–28020
Contact Anita Cook
Provides confidential informed support service for people who suffer from this disorder; maintains contacts by letter or telephone; runs a national network of local groups.

C P

Scoliosis Association

380–384 Harrow Road, London W9 2HU
01–289 5652
Contact Pauline Grey

Provides information and advice to parents of children with this condition; puts all people with this condition in touch with others similarly affected; campaigns for early screening of children to improve detection and treatment.
C B V P

Sickle Cell Society
Green Lodge, Barretts Green Road, London NW10 7AP
01–961 7795/8346
Contact Elizabeth Anionwu
Supports families and children affected by sickle cell disease; campaigns for improved services and for more treatment and research.
C B V P

Society for Advancement of Research into Anorexia
Stanthorpe, New Pound, Wisborough Green, West Sussex RH14 0EJ
0403–700210
Contact J M Jones/C R Jones
Promotes research into the causes, treatment and diagnosis of anorexia nervosa; raises funds.
C P

Society for Mucopolysaccharide Diseases
30 Westwood Drive, Little Chalfont, Bucks HP6 6RJ
02404–2789
Contact Christine Lavery
A support group for parents of children suffering from these diseases; runs an information and advice service; organises holidays for groups and families.
C B V P

Spare Tyre
86–88 Holmleigh Road, London N16 5PY
01–800 9099
Contact Katina Noble
Runs an information and advice

telephone line for women and girls with eating problems.

Tay-Sachs and Allied Diseases Association
17 Sydney Road, Barkingside, Ilford, Essex IG6 2ED
01–550 8989
Contact Alan Harris
Offers advice and counselling to parents of children with Tay-Sachs syndrome and allied conditions (Sandhoffs, Nieman-Pick etc). Raises funds for research and screening, and to purchase equipment to help affected children.
C

Terrence Higgins Trust
52–54 Grays Inn Road, London WC1X 8JU
01–831 0330 (administration)/ 01–242 1010 (helpline, 3-10 pm every day)
Contact Information Officer
Offers a wide range of welfare, legal and counselling help and support to people with AIDS, their families and friends; disseminates information about AIDS and provides health education for those at risk.
C V P

Tracheo-Oesophagal Fistula Support
124 Park Road, Chesterfield, Derbyshire S40 2LG
0246–237996
Contact Linda Morris
Promotes contact between families of children with this condition, provides information, arranges local support groups and a correspondence network.
C B V P

Tracheotomy Patients Aid Fund
70 Medway, Crowborough, East Sussex TN6 2DW
0896–652820
Contact R Shaw

Aims to improve the quality of intensive care patients permanently in need of ventilation. Raises funds in order to arrange for and provide portable ventilators for young patients who may be eligible for release into home care.
C

Tuberous Sclerosis Association of Great Britain

Little Barnsley Farm, Catshill, Bromsgrove, Worcs B61 0NQ
0572–71898
Contact Janet Medcalf
A self-help group for parents of children with this condition; shares problems, provides information, maintains contacts and sponsors research.
C P

United Kingdom Rett Syndrome Association

Freepost, Orpington, Kent BR5 1SZ
0689–26760
Contact Alison Clare
Offers parent-to-parent support, friendship, information and practical help to families who have a child suffering from this condition.
C B V P

United Kingdom Thalassaemia Society

107 Nightingale Lane, London N8 7QY
01–348 0437
Contact Christine Pericleous
Offers advice, support, information and counselling to people with this condition and their families.
C V P

Urostomy Association

'Buckland', Beaumont Park, Danbury, Essex CM3 4DE
024541–4294
Contact Angela Cooke
Provides information, care and support for people who have had this operation and their families; maintains a network of local support groups.
C B V

Vitiligo Group

PO Box 919, London SE21 8AW
01–670 7175
Offers information, support and advice to people with this condition.
C B V P

LEISURE

CAMPAIGNING ORGANISATIONS

Fair Play for Children Association
West View, Mines Avenue, Aigburth, Liverpool L17 6AL
Contact Tony Dronfield
Campaigns for more, better and safer play facilities and services for children. Provides advice and information on all matters relating to children's play facilities.
C P

Friends of the Earth
26/28 Underwood Street, London N1 7QJ
01–490 1555
Campaigns on a wide range of environmental issues; maintains network of about 250 local groups, with local activities; produces educational materials.
C B V P

Groundwork *see* p.99

Play for Life
31b Ipswich Road, Norwich NR2 2LN
0603–505947
Contact Josephine Rado
Encourages fresh thinking about the play experience of children; supplies resource material and information, arranges exhibitions.
C V P

CHILDREN'S AND YOUNG PEOPLE'S ORGANISATIONS

GENERAL

Air Training Corps (ATC)
Headquarters Air Cadets, RAF Newton, Nottingham NG1 8RH
0949–20771 ext 441 (Public Relations Office)
Contact Air Officer Commanding Headquarters Air Cadets
Aims to encourage a practical interest in aviation and the Royal Air Force among young men and women from 13–22 years. Provides training in leadership and good citizenship, adventure activities and opportunities for travel.
B V P

Association for Christian Youth Work
113 Loveday Road, London W13 9JU
01–567 7718
Contact Rev Bruce C Porter
Organises local groups, each offering a wide range of activities for children and young people.
C B V P

Association of Combined Youth Clubs
579 Battersea Park Road, London SW11 3BH
01–228 9143
Contact Ernie R Randall
Encourages the formation and development of local junior and youth groups within neighbourhood

communities, and assists in the running of these clubs.
C B V P

Boys' Brigade

1 King's Terrace, Galena Road, Hammersmith, London W12 0LT
01–741 4001
Contact Information Officer
A Christian organisation which runs educational and recreational programmes for boys aged 6–18, in separate groups according to age. Activities include leadership training, adventure pursuits, community interests and sports.
C B V P

Church Lads' and Church Girls' Brigade

2 Barnsley Road, Wath-upon-Dearne, Rotherham, S.Yorks S63 6PY
0709–876535
Contact Rev Charles Grice
Brigade companies, attached to local Anglican churches, provide educational, training, and recreational activities for children and young people.
C B V

Crusaders Union

2 Romeland Hill, St Albans, Herts AL3 4ET
0272–55422
Contact Heather Keep
Christian children's and youth organisation. Local groups organise weekly meetings for games, activities and Bible reading. Over 70 adventure holidays provided nationally and a wide range of leadership training events.
C B V P

Forest School Camps

110 Burbage Road, London SE24 9HD
01–274 7566
Contact Lorna English

Arranges educational and recreational camps for children (including those with mental or physical disability) aged 6–17. Camps are designed to foster self-reliance and responsibility, sympathy and tolerance, and an understanding of the countryside.
C B V P

Girl Guides Association

17–19 Buckingham Palace Road, London SW1W 0PT
01–836 6242
Contact Information Officer
A voluntary movement for girls, Rainbows (5–7), Brownies (7–11), Guides (10–14), Rangers (14–18), Young Leaders (15–18) and Adult Leaders, which aims to help its members to achieve their own fullest physical, emotional, mental and spiritual development in order that they may make their best contribution to the world in which they live.
C B V P

Girls' Brigade

Girls' Brigade House, Foxhall Road, Didcot, Oxon OX11 7BQ
0235–510425
Contact Audrey Rowland
A Christian organisation; groups are attached to local churches. Girls receive religious instruction, and take part in a wide variety of activities, educational, recreational, and to benefit the community.
C B V

Girls Friendly Society and Townsend Fellowship

126 Queen's Gate, London SW7 5LQ
01–589 9628
Contact General Secretary
An Anglican organisation; aims to promote spiritual and personal development and to give service to the church and the community.

Arranges educational, recreational and leadership training activities. Runs residential hostels.
C B V P

Girls Venture Corps Air Cadets

Redhill Aerodrome, Kingsmill Lane, South Nutfield, Redhill, Surrey RH1 5JY
0737–832245
A non-political, non-denominational organisation for girls aged 13–20, which provides training for character, mind and body, and encourages service to the community. Arranges flying experience and gives scholarships for pilot training. Arranges outdoor adventure activities, sports and travel.

Methodist Association of Youth Clubs

2 Chester House, Pages Lane, London N10 1PR
01–444 9845
Organises fellowships, youth clubs, open centres, discussion groups, gospel groups and sports activities for young people; works with young employed people; undertakes volunteering projects, international exchanges and evangelism.
C B P V

Methodist Church Division of Education and Youth

2 Chester House, Pages Lane, London N10 1PR
01–444 9845
Gives assistance and advice to all sections of youth and children's activity in churches, colleges and schools.
C P

National Association of Boys' Clubs

369 Kennington Lane, London SE11 5QY
01–793 0787
Contact Michael Orbell

Maintains and develops a network of clubs for boys throughout the UK. Co-ordinates a wide-ranging programme of educational, recreational and sporting activities.
C B V P

National Council for Voluntary Youth Services

Wellington House, 29 Albion Street, Leicester LE1 6GD
0533–471400
A co-ordinating body which represents most national voluntary youth organisations, and maintains links with the network of local councils for voluntary youth service throughout the country.
C B P

National Federation of Young Farmers' Clubs

YFC Centre, National Agricultural Centre, Kenilworth, Warks CV8 2LG
0203–696544
Contact B P Shields
Co-ordinates the activities of Young Farmers' Clubs in England and Wales, for young people aged 10–26. YFCs arrange recreational and educational events, including conservation, sports, fundraising, international exchanges, competitions and social gatherings.
B V P

National Out of School Alliance

Oxford House, Derbyshire Street, London E2 1HG
01–739 4787/7870
Contact Colette Mercer
Supports and encourages community-based 'out of school' schemes, and local authority projects in schools, youth clubs, etc, through advice, training and research.
C B V P

National Playbus Association

Unit G, Arno's Castle Estate, Junction Road, Brislington, Bristol BS4 5AJ
0272–775375
Contact Duncan Bowling
An umbrella organisation which encourages the use of mobile community resources (playbuses etc). Provides advice, grants and information; runs training schemes.
C B V P

National Youth Bureau

17–23 Albion Street, Leicester LE1 6GD
0533–471200
Contact Jackie Scott
Provides information and advice to parent volunteers and professionals involved in youth work.
C P

Scout Association

Baden-Powell House, Queen's Gate, London SW7 5JS
01–584 7030
Contact Relationships Secretary
Aims to encourage the mental, physical and spiritual development of young people so that they may take a constructive place in society; runs local groups for boys and a wide range of outdoor pursuits, cultural and community service activities.
C B V P

Sea Cadet Association

202 Lambeth Road, London SE1 7JE
01–928 8978
Supports the activities of the Sea Cadets, a national voluntary youth organisation.
C B V

Sea Cadet Corps

202 Lambeth Road, London SE1 7JF
01–928 8978
Offers sea-training, sports,

recreational and social activities to boys and girls aged 12-18.
C B V P

Sea Ranger Association

HQTS Lord Amory, Dollar Bay, 301 Marsh Wall, London E14 9TF
01–987 1757
Contact Vera Corner Halligan
Promotes the training for good citizenship of girls of all races and creeds, especially in outdoor and nautical activities.
C B V

Woodcraft Folk

13 Ritherdon Road, London SW17 8QE
01–672 6031/767 2457
Contact Information Officer
A youth organisation concerned to foster the principles of universal tolerance, equality and friendship. Runs weekly meetings for children aged 6-16, organised by volunteer parents, and arranges numerous recreational, cultural and outdoor activities, as well as exchanges with similar groups overseas.
C B V P

Youth Clubs – UK

Keswick House, 30 Peacock Lane, Leicester LE1 5NY
0533–29514
Contact Jan Holt
Maintains a network of 45 local associations which run clubs for young people, designed to encourage them to use their leisure activities to develop their physical, mental and spiritual capacities to the full.
C B V P

Youth Hostels Association (England and Wales)

Trevelyan House, St Albans, Herts AL1 2DY
0272–55215
Contact Information Department

Encourages knowledge, love and care of the countryside; provides hostels where young people can stay for a limited time.
C B V P

SPECIAL GROUPS

Association for Jewish Youth
50 Lindley Street, London E1 3AX
01–790 6407
Contact Helen Rose
Runs a centralised programme of sporting and cultural events for Jewish young people, together with a voluntary youth service. Trains voluntary and professional youth leaders; offers consultancy service.
C V B P

Community Action Projects
Goodricke College, York University, Heslington, York YO1 5DD
0904–412328
Runs camps for disadvantaged children from the north of England, and various term-time projects.
C B V P

Jewish Lads and Girls Brigade
3 Beechcroft, South Woodford, London E18 1LA
01–989 8990
Contact Charles Kay
Aims to train members in loyalty, honour, discipline and self-respect, so that they may become a credit to their country and their community.
Arranges a variety of sporting, recreational and educational activities.
C B V P

National Association of Asian Youth
see under FAMILY WELFARE, p.35

National Federation of Gateway Clubs
see under HANDICAP, p.49

Organisation for Black Arts Advancement and Learning Activities
see p.96

Union of Maccabi Associations in Great Britain and Northern Ireland
Atlas House, 190 Iverson Road, London NW6 2HL
01–328 0382
Contact Beryl Rayman
Maintains an affiliation of Jewish youth clubs throughout the country, and organises educational, recreational, sporting and cultural activities for young people.
C B V P

ORGANISATIONS TO IMPROVE LEISURE FACILITIES

Festival Welfare Services
c/o NCHR, 15 Britannia Street, London WC1X 9JP
01–837 2509
Contact Penny Mellor
Co-ordinates welfare services, including first aid and medical, emotional and legal counselling, at pop festivals and open-air concerts.
C V P

Free Form Arts Trust Ltd
38 Dalston Lane, London E8 3AZ
01–249 3394
Runs a Community Arts in Education programme; helps design imaginative gardens, play areas etc. Provides information, exhibition materials, speakers.
C V P

National Centre for Play
see under EDUCATION, p.4

National Federation of Community Organisations
see under EDUCATION, p.2

Play Matters/The National Toy Libraries Association

68 Churchway, London NW1 1LT
01–387 9592
Contact Lesley Houlston
Toy libraries lend the best (and sometimes specially-adapted) toys to all children, including those with special needs. They aim to provide support, advice and friendship for parents. The Association brings together professionals – therapists, teachers, psychologists – and volunteers, and liaises with the toy trade. Gives guidance about setting up and running toy libraries.
C B V P

Scout and Guide Association

29 The Green, Huthwaite, Sutton in Ashfield, Notts NG17 2RP
Contact Elizabeth Davis-Johns
Maintains a network of professional people with experience of the Scout and Guide movement, and who are ready to assist projects connected with it; runs study groups/workshops, organises camps, practical activities and social events.
C B

ORGANISATIONS FOR SPECIFIC ACTIVITIES

ADVENTURE

Operation Raleigh (The Scientific Exploration Society Ltd)

Operation Raleigh Central Headquarters, Alpha Place, Flood Street, London SW3 5SZ
01–351 7541
Contact Alison Blythe-Brook
Runs a development programme for 17–25 year olds involving expeditions to selected world sites to engage in scientific and community work and adventure.
C B V P

Outward Bound Trust

Chestnut Field, Regent Place, Rugby CV21 2PJ
0788–60423
Contact Janet Smith
Organises short outdoor adventure courses to present young people with tasks and challenges that encourage them to realise their own potential, take initiatives and gain in self-confidence.
C B P

Project Trust

Breacachadh Castle, Isle of Coll, Argyll, Scotland
08793–444
Contact Major Nicholas Bristol
Arranges working visits overseas (mainly in developing countries) for young people (17–19), to further their education and experience. Applications to go overseas in September should be received by the preceding 1st January.
C

Young Explorers Trust

c/o Royal Geographical Society, 1 Kensington Gore, London SW7 2AR
01–589 9724
Contact Hon Secretary
Aims to increase the opportunities for young people to take part in interesting ventures in remote areas, both in this country and abroad. Gives advice and training to expedition leaders. Runs network of local groups.
C B V P

ARTS AND LEARNING

Amateur Music Association

Medlock Junior School, Wadeson Road, Manchester M13 9UR
Contact Ian Clarke
Encourages all forms of amateur music-making throughout the UK. Runs an information centre,

co-ordinates promotional projects such as the 'Get Back to Music' campaign.
C V P

Benslow Music Trust
Little Benslow Hills, Benslow Lane, Hitchin, Herts SG4 9RB
0462–55175/59446
Contact Rachel Ward
Holds residential courses for amateur musicians and teachers. Runs a musical instrument loan scheme for young musicians and students.
C V P

British Federation of Music Festivals
Festivals House, 198 Park Lane, Macclesfield, Cheshire SK11 6UD
0625–28297
Runs amateur music festivals which offer a platform for performers of all ages, although 80% are under 18. Organises an annual instrumental summer school for young players.
C B V P

British Federation of Young Choirs
Loughborough College, Radmoor, Loughborough, Leics LE11 3BT
Contact Susan Lansdale
Holds international singing weeks and weekends for young singers and choirs; runs training courses for choirs and their teachers; offers grant aid and advice to individuals and choirs.
C V B P

British Philatelic Trust
British Philatelic Centre, 107 Charterhouse Street, London EC1M 6PT
01–251 5040
Contact J D B Littlebury
Produces handbooks and catalogues suitable for use in school stamp clubs.
C P

British Puppet and Model Theatre Guild
18 Maple Road, Yeading, Hayes Middx UB4 9LP
Contact Percy Press 01–802 4656
A group of serious model-makers; organises festivals and exhibitions, weekend schools; offers advice, can provide technical information sheets.
B V P

Central Council for Amateur Theatre
Regent's College, Regent's Park, London NW1 4NW
01–935 2571
Contact Sally Meades
Can put parents in touch with local amateur theatrical groups with activities for children.

Community Music Ltd
15 Wilkin Street, London NW5 5SG
01–485 8553
Contact Charlie Inskip
Aims to provide a comprehensive and accessible music service with a particular emphasis on education, training and information. Runs free music information service; encourages new musical education ventures.
C V P

Council for Music in Hospitals
340 Lower Road, Little Bookham, Surrey KT23 4EF
0372–58264
Contact Sylvia Lindsay
Arranges performances of live music in hospitals, residential homes, hospices etc, to improve the quality of life for residents. Parents of children in hospital etc may ask for concerts to be arranged, or for advice on arranging performances.
C

Dance for Everyone

6 Milverton Road, London NW6 7AS
01–451 2000
Contact Jan Moriarty
Arranges workshops and performances in schools and theatres in London and the Home Counties. Specialises in working with children with special needs and with deaf people.
C V

English Folk Song and Dance Society

Cecil Sharp House, 2 Regent's Park Road, London NW1 7AY
01–485 2206
Aims to preserve and make known English folk songs, dances and other folk music; has educational programme; maintains strong links with education authorities and schools; can inform parents of local folk dance groups which accept children.
C B P

Faculty of Church Music

316 Bath Road, Worcester WR5 3ET
Contact Rev Dr P Faunch,
7 Whitknots Way, Caterham, Surrey
Promotes high standards in church music, including choirs where boys and girls sing. Arranges tuition and an examinations scheme.
V

Federation of Astronomical Societies

1 Tal-y-Bont Road, Ely, Cardiff, Wales CF5 5EU
Contact Christine G Sheldon
An umbrella organisation co-ordinating the activities of various local astronomical societies and groups. May be able to tell parents about local groups which admit young members.
B V P

Federation of Family History Societies

The Benson Room, c/o The Birmingham and Midland Institute, Margaret Street, Birmingham B3 3BS
021–705 6078
Co-ordinates and assists the work of local groups and other bodies interested in family history. Maintains a reference collection, publishes helpful literature for researchers.
C B V P

Festival of Chinese Arts

PO Box 892, London NW1 0NF
Contact Chairperson
Provides a forum for Chinese cultural activities, mainly in London; encourages events and activities based on Chinese themes and traditional festivals.

Horizon Dance Group

83 Belgrade Road, London N16 8DH
Contact Ronen Dam
A dance education centre for children which aims to promote a better understanding among 4–12 year olds of different social and cultural backgrounds.

Imperial Society of Teachers of Dancing

Euston Hall, Birkenhead Street, London WC1H 8BE
Contact Jean Rush
01–837 9967
Aims to promote the knowledge of dance, and to maintain and improve teaching standards and techniques. Offers advice to parents on dancing schools and teachers; gives careers guidance.
C P

InterChange

15 Wilkin Street, London NW5 3NG
01–267 9421
Contact Alan Tomkins
A national agency concerned to

encourage a wide range of community-based projects, including performance arts courses for young people.
C B P

Live Music Now

15 Grosvenor Gardens, London SW1W 0BD
01–828 7073
Contact Virginia Renshaw
Aims to provide performance opportunities to talented young professional musicians, and to bring the experience of live music back into everyday life, by means of concerts in hospitals, hospices, schools, prisons, residential care homes and centres for homeless people.
C B V

National Association of Arts Centres

Room 110, The Arts Centre, Vane Terrace, Darlington, DL3 7AX
0325–465930
Contact Rick Welton
The representative body for organisations working in the arts at a local level; provides information about arts opportunities and projects for parents and children; can advise on arts education projects in schools; publishes information books.
P

National Association of Youth Orchestras

Ainslie House, 11 Colme Street, Edinburgh EH3 6AG
031–225 4606
Contact Carol Main
An umbrella organisation, representing youth orchestras and fostering their development. Organises annual festivals, competitions, exchange visits. Can provide information about local youth orchestras.
C V P

National Youth Choir of Great Britain

PO Box 67, Holmfirth, West Yorkshire HD7 1GQ
0484–687023
Contact Sue Christie
The National Youth Choir is made up of young singers between the ages of 15–21 who are auditioned from various parts of the country. Singers attend courses and give concerts, make recordings and go on tours.
C V

National Youth Orchestra of Great Britain

Suite A, Causeway House, Lodge Causeway, Bristol BS16 3HD
0272–650036
Contact Linda M Andrew
Can provide parents with information on how their children can apply to join the orchestra, the standards of playing required, etc.
C V P

Organisation for Black Arts Advancement and Learning Activities

Obaala House, 225 Seven Sisters Road, London N4 2DA
01–263 1918 (administration); 01–263 8016 (live arts)
Contact Gretchen Cummings
Runs a variety of Black artistic projects, including an art gallery, a specialist art bookshop, the Obaala Poetry Theatre, a summer art school, and educational and creative activities for Black children aged 11–16. Offers information and advice to artists, administrators and community groups.

Royal Academy of Dancing

48 Vicarage Crescent, London SW11 3LT
01–223 0091
Contact Registrar
Can provide information about ballet

classes for children run by trained teachers, and about training courses, summer schools and classes for teachers of ballet.
C B P

Society of Genealogists
14 Charterhouse Buildings, Goswell Road, London EC1M 7BA
01–251 8799
Contact Anthony Camp
Provides facilities for students of family history; maintains a library and archive collections; promotes reseach.
C V P

COMMUNITY SERVICE

Community Projects Foundation
60 Highbury Grove, London N5 2AG
01–226 5375
Seeks to establish innovative community development and youth work projects. Provides information and advice. Current concerns include rural community work, young offenders.
C B

Community Service Volunteers
237 Pentonville Road, London N1 9NJ
01–278 6601
Contact Sean Jefferson
Young (16–35) full-time volunteers work for 4–12 months with people in need. Food, accommodation and £18 a week provided. CSV encourages community involvement in education through publications, training and local projects. Youth employment schemes involve young unemployed people in training and work of community benefit.
C B P

Councils for Voluntary Service – National Association
26 Bedford Square, London WC1B 3HU
01–636 4066
Contact Information Officer
Organising body for councils for voluntary service (CVS) throughout Britain. Can provide information for parents wanting to find out what volunteer schemes operate in their area.
C B V P

Project Trust
see p.93

Royal Life Saving Society
Mountbatten House, Studley, Warks B80 7NN
052785–3943
Contact Shaun Whatling
Teaches water safety, water rescue and resuscitation techniques. Has links with schools and swimming clubs throughout the UK.
C B V P

St John Ambulance
1 Grosvenor Crescent, London SW1X 7EF
01–235 5231
Contact John Mills
Organises volunteers who are trained to save life, care for the sick and injured and relieve suffering. Runs junior section ('Badgers') with a wide-ranging programme of activities including first aid.
C B V P

Time for God Scheme
2 Chester House, Pages Lane, London N10 1PR
01–883 1504
Contact Penelope Prestage
Provides opportunities for voluntary service for young people, in community and welfare work, or work within churches.
C V

Youth Development Association
The Derker Annexe Centre, Derker Street, Oldham, Lancs
061–633 0593
Contact Christine Edgar
Encourages independent voluntary youth work; provides practical help and support for local groups.
B V P

CONSERVATION

British Association for Local History
Shopwycke Hall, Chichester, West Sussex PO20 6BQ
0234–787639
Contact Gill Lowden
Organises local history courses and visits; produces publications.
C V P

British Hedgehog Preservation Society
Knowbury House, Knowbury, Ludlow, Shropshire SY8 3LQ
Contact Leslie Sharp
Aims to protect hedgehogs and to encourage children to respect all wildlife. Answers postal enquiries; provides information and educational materials; sends lecturers to schools, local groups etc.
C P

British Naturalists' Association
69 Marloes, Hemel Hempstead, Herts
Contact General Secretary, 48 Russell Way, Higham Ferrers, Northants NN9 8EJ
Holds national and local meetings, field trips at home and abroad and exhibitions; runs an information service; holds an annual competition for young people; publishes study guides.
C B V P

British Ornithologists' Union
c/o British Museum (Natural History), Sub-department of Ornithology, Tring, Herts HP23 6AP
0442–890080
Contact Gwen Bonham
Aims to foster links between professional and amateur ornithologists.
C P

British Trust for Conservation Volunteers
36 St Mary Street, Wallingford, Oxon OX10 0EU
0491–39766
Contact Jane Bevan
Organises practical conservation work by volunteers throughout the UK. Works with schools to introduce conservation work as part of the curriculum.
C B V P

British Trust for Ornithology
Beech Grove, Tring, Herts HP23 5NR
0442–823461
Contact Beth Smith
Researches Britain's birds. Professional staff liaise with amateurs throughout the country.
C B V P

Cathedral Camps
Manor House, High Birstwith, Harrogate, North Yorks HG3 2LG
Contact Maud Holliday 0432–771850
Runs summer camps where volunteers can work together to help conserve and restore cathedral buildings and their surroundings.
C

Common Ground
45 Shelton Street, London WC2H 9HJ
01–379 3109
Gives advice and encouragement to local groups (mainly, though not exclusively, of adults) interested in conserving the environment and the

heritage of the past. Supports community arts initiatives with an environmental theme.
C V P

Council for British Archaeology
112 Kennington Road, London SE11 6RE
01–582 0494
Contact Gillian Heyworth
Encourages archaeological research; organises excavations where young (16+) people may work as volunteers; produces educational materials about archaeology.

Field Studies Council
Preston Montford, Montford Bridge, Shrewsbury SY4 1HW
0743–850674
Contact Anthony Thomas
Runs environmental educational courses for all ages at nine residential centres. Programme available.
C V B P

Friends of the Earth
see p.88

Groundwork
Bennetts Court, 6 Bennetts Hill, Birmingham B2 5ST
021–236 8565
Contact Sally Wilkinson
Aims to promote the improvement and care of the urban environment and its rural fringe for the benefit of the population as a whole through a national network of local Groundwork trusts. Some of the projects set up by these trusts have involved participation by children, schools, community groups, industry etc.
C B V P

London Wildlife Trust
80 York Way, London N1 9AG
Contact (for WATCH) Sue Wyatt
Promotes a wide variety of nature conservation projects within the

Greater London Area, and encourages a greater awareness of the value of wildlife beyond the urban setting. Runs a junior group called WATCH.
C B V P

Mammal Society
Baltic Exchange Buildings, 21 Bury Street, London EC3A 5AU
01–283 1266
Contact Dr J S Churchfield
Promotes interest in, and the study of, mammals, by professionals and amateurs. Runs a youth section.
C V P

National Federation of City Farms
The Old Vicarage, 66 Fraser Street, Bedminster, Bristol BS3 4YL
0272–660663
Contact Ian Egginton-Metters
Promotes and supports city farm and community garden projects throughout the UK; can offer ideas and skills, help with on-site fieldwork, fundraising, and development work.
C B V P

National Trust for Places of Historic Interest or Natural Beauty
36 Queen Anne's Gate, London SW1H 9AS
01–222 9251
Works to preserve, for the benefit of the nation, buildings of architectural importance or historic interest, and coastlines and countryside of beauty. Runs educational activities at several of its properties; maintains a youth section.
C B V P

Royal Society for the Protection of Birds
The Lodge, Sandy, Beds SG19 2DL
0767–80551
Contact Inquiry Officer
Works to conserve birds and the places where they breed and live. Runs Young Ornithologists' Club (over

100,000 members); supplies information and advice; maintains network of local groups.
C B V P

Urban Wildlife Group
131–133 Sherlock Street, Birmingham, B5 6NB
021–666 7474
Contact Tom Slater
Aims to increase awareness of wildlife among young people; provides range of educational services.
C P

Watch Trust for Environmental Education
22 The Green, Nettleham, Lincoln LN2 2NR
0522–752326
Contact Simon Perry or Wayne Talbot
Aims to educate young people in an understanding and appreciation of the natural environment; organises practical conservation projects for children and a national environmental club for young people.
C B V P

WWF-UK
Panda House, Wayside Park, Godalming, Surrey GU7 1XR
Contact Information Officer
Raises money for the conservation of endangered wild animals and plants, and promotes the wise use of world natural resources. Runs youth membership scheme, produces educational materials.
C B V P

Young Peoples' Trust for the Environment
95 Woodbridge Road, Guildford, Surrey GU1 4PY
0483–39600
Contact Information Officer
Aims to educate young people in all matters relating to conservation; runs

an information service for schools and individuals, and various wildlife study courses.
C B V P

READING

Books for Keeps
1 Effingham Road, Lee, London SE12 8NZ
01–852 4953
Contact Richard Hill
Publishes a magazine of reviews of children's books, plus a number of guides on books for children. Can provide information and answer telephone enquiries.
P

Letterbox Library
8 Broadway, London N16 8JN
01–254 1640
A book club for parents and children, specialising in anti-sexist and multicultural children's books; stock is mainly hardback which is sold at a discount. Newsletter and catalogues to members.
V

National Committee on Racism in Children's Books
see under EDUCATION, p.6

National Listening Library
12 Lant Street, London SE1 1QH
01–407 9417
Contact Marina Smith
Provides a library of books on tape for use by patients in hospital who are unable to read for themselves.
C P

SPORT

Association for Archery in Schools
Bloxham School, Banbury, Oxon OX15 4PE
0295–720443

Contact Chris Fletcher-Campbell
Promotes archery in schools and
other educational institutions;
organises coaching, awards,
tournaments and championships.
V B P

Backpackers Club

PO Box 381, 7–10 Friar Street,
Reading, Berks RG3 4RL
Contact Dr Eric R Gurney
Represents the interests of people
who take part in a variety of outdoor
pursuits; encourages the full use of
established footpaths and open areas.
B V P

Badminton Association of England

National Badminton Centre, Bradwell
Road, Loughton Lodge, Milton
Keynes, MK8 9LA
0908–568822
Contact Jake Donney
The organising body for the sport of
badminton in England; encourages
the teaching of badminton in schools.
B V P

British BMX Association

Beverly Building, 61 Bryn Street,
Ashton in Makerfield, Wigan
WN4 9AX
0942–721491
Can provide information on local clubs
and race meetings for children; also
arranges accident insurance for
members.

British Cycling Federation

36 Rockingham Road, Kettering,
Northants NN16 8HG
0536–412211
Aims to encourage, promote, develop
and control the sport and pastime of
cycling; runs an information service
about cycling.
V P

British Horse Society

British Equestrian Centre, Stoneleigh,
Kenilworth, Warks CV8 2LR
0203–696697
Contact Ceri Burgum
Acts as the governing body for a wide
variety of adult competitions involving
horses. Provides riding and road
safety tuition. Can advise on the
welfare of horses, access, and rights
of way.
C B V P

British Judo Association

9 Islington High Street, London
N1 9LQ
01–833 4424
Can provide information about local
classes for children and adults.
Governing body for licensed clubs
with qualified instructors.

British Olympic Association

1 Wandsworth Plain, London
SW18 1EH
01–871 2677
Contact Information Officer
The official body organising British
participation in the Olympic Games.
Produces educational and publicity
material.
V P

British Speedway Supporters Club

52 Byron Avenue, Manor Park,
London E12 6NG
01–471 6142
Contact Ron Dyer
Aims to help new young speedway
riders, and to answer enquiries
concerning the sport.

Central Council of Physical Recreation

Francis House, Francis Street, London
SW1P 1DE
01–832 3163
Contact Amanda Sabin
Can provide information on how to
contact the governing or

representative bodies of a large number of sports played in the UK, to enable parents to find out what local groups and facilities exist.

Cirdan Trust

31 Imperial Avenue, Maylandsea, Chelmsford, Essex CM3 6AH
0621–740943
To help educate young people through participation aboard large sailing vessels. Provides training and instruction.
C V P

English Basketball Association

Calomax House, Lupton Avenue, Leeds LS9 6EE
0532–496044
Contact Brian Aldred
The governing body of the sport in England. Can supply information about junior clubs in the regions.

Fairbridge Drake Society (Inc)

Suite 25–31 Chancery House, 53–64 Chancery Lane, London WC2A 1QX
01–831 7858/01–242 6748
Aims to motivate young, unemployed people in the UK, through a programme of adventurous outdoor activities and skills training, towards employment or some other constructive use of their time.
C B V

Martial Arts Commission

3rd Floor, Broadway House, 15/16 Deptford Broadway, London SE8 4PE
01–691 3433
Can provide information about licensed martial arts clubs for children, with qualified instructors.

National Council for Schools' Sports

see under EDUCATION, p.14

National Playing Fields Association

25 Ovington Square, London SW3 1LQ
01–584 6445
Contact Tony Watson
Provides help, advice and information to individuals or groups wishing to preserve, improve or acquire recreational facilities for the benefit of the community, particularly for children and young people.
C

National Skating Association of Great Britain

15–27 Gee Street, London EC1V 3RE
01–253 3824
Can provide information about local tuition in ice-skating by qualified instructors.

Sail Training Organisation

2a The Hard, Portsmouth, Hants PO1 3PT
0705–832055/6
Contact Bruce Donald
Arranges short adventure voyages for young people (16-24) on board two 300-tonne schooners; participates in Cutty Sark Tall Ships Race.
C B V P

Sports Council

16 Upper Woburn Place, London WC1H 0QT
Can give general advice and information about sport, including participation and careers.
P

United Kingdom Sports Association for People with a Mental Handicap

see under HANDICAP, p.50

TRAVEL

British Association of the Experiment in International Living

Otesaga, West Malvern Road, Malvern, Worcs WR14 4EN
0684–562577
Arranges exchange visits between UK residents and nationals from other countries; organises homestays in the UK for overseas visitors.
C B V P

Central Bureau

Seymour Mews House, Seymour Mews, London W1H 9PE
01–486 5101
Contact Carole Bevis
Publishes guides covering opportunities for holiday jobs, voluntary work, language courses, exchanges and homestays in Britain and abroad, plus a series of guides for young travellers. Administers educational and vocational exchange schemes for teachers, students, young people and schools.
C P

Children's Country Holidays Fund

1 York Street, Baker Street, London W1H 1PZ
01–935 8371/3/4
Arranges country holidays for inner-city children aged 5–13 years for whom no other holidays are available.
C V

Intercultural Exchange Programmes

see under EDUCATION, p.4

How to contact voluntary organisations

If you would like more detailed information about any of the voluntary organisations mentioned in this directory, please write to the organisation concerned, ENCLOSING A LARGE STAMPED ADDRESSED ENVELOPE. Postage can be a very heavy burden for voluntary organisations. If you do not pre-pay the postage, they may not be able to afford to reply to your letter.

Information about national voluntary organisations may be obtained from the Intelligence and Information Unit at the National Council for Voluntary Organisations, 26 Bedford Square, London WC1B 3HU, telephone 01–636 4066.

For information about community-based self-help organisations, contact the National Federation of Self-Help Organisations, 150 Townmead Road, London SW6 2RA, telephone 01–731 8440.

Information about local voluntary organisations, and about local schemes for volunteering, may be available from your local library or from community workers or the social services department at your local town hall. The following organisations may also be able to help you: your local Council for Voluntary Service (address from Councils for Voluntary Service – National Association, 26 Bedford Square, London WC1B 3HU, telephone 01–636 4066) or your local Citizens Advice Bureau (address in phone book).

For information about voluntary organisations in Scotland, Wales and Northern Ireland, contact the following bodies:

Scottish Council for Voluntary Organisations
18–19 Claremont Crescent, Edinburgh
EH7 4QD
031–556 3882

Wales Council for Voluntary Action
Llys Ifor, Crescent Road, Caerffili, Canol
Morgannwg CF8 1XL
0222–869224

Northern Ireland Council for Voluntary Action
127 Ormeau Road, Belfast BT7 1SH
0232–321224

Organisations which can help you set up a new group

The following organisations may be able to help you with advice and information about setting up a new voluntary organisation to meet your local needs. They may also produce useful publications for sale:

Action Resource Centre
CAP House, 9–12 Long Lane, London
EC1A 9HD
01–726 8987

Charities Advisory Trust
Radius Works, Back Lane, London NW3 1HL
01–794 9835

Charities Aid Foundation
48 Pembury Road, Tonbridge, Kent TN9 2JD
0732–356323

Charity Commission
St Alban's House, 57–60 Haymarket, London
SW1Y 4QX
01–210 3000

Councils for Voluntary Service – National
   Association
26 Bedford Square, London WC1B 3HU
01–636 4066

Directory of Social Change
Radius Works, Back Lane, London NW3 1HL
01–435 8171

Inter-Action Trust
Royal Victoria Dock, London E16 1BT
01–511 0411

National Council for Voluntary Organisations
26 Bedford Square, London WC1B 3HU
01–636 4066

National Federation of Community
   Organisations
8–9 Upper Street, London N1 0PQ
01–226 0189

National Federation of Self-Help
   Organisations
150 Townmead Road, London SW6 2RA
01–731 8440

Self-Help Alliance
29 Lower King's Road, Berkhamstead, Herts
HP4 2AB
04427–73311

Volunteer Centre
29 Lower King's Road, Berkhamstead, Herts
HP4 2AB
04427–73311

It might also be worth writing to organisations listed in this directory (remember to enclose an SAE) who appear to share some of your own aims and objectives, to see whether they have any useful tips to pass on.

Index of names

FORM FOR NEW DIRECTORY ENTRIES

If you would like your organisation to be considered for inclusion in the next edition of this directory, please complete the form below and return it, or a photocopy, to:

Co-ordinator, BSP Directories Series
Bedford Square Press/NCVO
26 Bedford Square
London WC1B 3HU

ALL ENTRIES IN THE DIRECTORY ARE FREE

Name of Organisation   ....

Address   ....

....

Telephone Number   ....

Person to Contact   ....

BRIEF (no more than 50 words) description of the services/information/ advice your organisation can offer to PARENTS. (NB We do NOT need a complete account of the full range of services your organisation can provide.)

....

....

....

....

....

....

Are you a charity?   Yes/No
Do you have branches/local groups?   Yes/No
Do you use volunteers in your work?   Yes/No
Do you produce publications?   Yes/No

Signature   ....

Position   ....

Date   ....

NCVO/BSP give permission for the above form to be photocopied

THE VOLUNTARY AGENCIES DIRECTORY

THE SOCIAL ACTIVISTS' BIBLE

NCVO's directory of voluntary agencies is the standard reference work for anyone who cares about helping the community. It lists nearly 2,000 leading voluntary agencies, ranging from small, specialist self-help groups to long-established national charities. It gives concise, up-to-date descriptions of their aims and activities, with details of

charitable status	local branches
volunteer participation	membership
trading activities	staffing

A list of useful addresses includes professional and public advisory bodies concerned with voluntary action; a classified index and quick reference list of acronyms and abbreviations give easy access to entries.

There is extensive coverage of new groups concerned with women's issues, minority rights, self-help, community development and leisure activities, environment and conservation, campaigning and consumer affairs.

Voluntary agencies play an important part in making the world a better place to live in. This NCVO directory is the essential guide to their work.

'If you buy only one directory of voluntary agencies, buy this one and buy it every year.' *Health Libraries Review*

'an essential working tool' *Environment Now*

Sponsored by Charity Recruitment

FORTHCOMING

THE HEALTH DIRECTORY

Compiled by Fiona Macdonald

Published in association with Thames Television

Thames Television's Help! Programme receives daily enquiries from patients and their families for information on how to cope with many common (and not so common) health problems. Whether you live in the London area, and watch the Help! programme, or whether you live elsewhere in the UK, *The Health Directory* can help you and your family.

This new expanded and updated edition lists almost 800 organisations, including well-known national bodies and advice services as well as informal self-help groups. The entries are listed alphabetically, covering a wide range of problems. Whether you want the Association for Post-Natal Illness, CancerLink, Incontinence Advisory Service, Motor Neurone Disease Association, Sickle Cell Society, or even Yoga for Health Foundation you can find them all here.

Most are London-based. Many have branches elsewhere. All will help you with your enquiries. Doctors, nurses and other professional health workers will find the directory a useful reference tool.

'It has taken its place on my desk amongst the essential information literature. Invaluable!' *Health and Healing*

CHILDREN ARE PEOPLE TOO

THE CASE AGAINST PHYSICAL PUNISHMENT
PETER NEWELL

Hitting people is wrong – and children are people too.

The current explosion of concern over child abuse has tragically drawn attention to how children are treated by adults. Peter Newell's campaigning book, written from a children's rights perspective, draws together for the first time all the arguments for ending the physical punishment of children by their parents and other carers.

The aim, the author argues, is to improve the status of children and to reduce violence, including child abuse. He proposes that children should have the same legal protection as adults do from all forms of assault. In support of his case, he describes the positive effects of the reforms which have prohibited all hitting of children in Sweden, Finland, Denmark, Norway and most recently Austria.

Children Are People Too summarises the arguments against hitting children – the fundamental injustice, the risk of injury, links with more serious child abuse, with aggression, delinquency, etc.; assesses the prevalence of physical punishment in the UK and other countries; and sets out the current legal framework and how it should be changed. It also documents the long struggle to end school corporal punishment in the UK.

Peter Newell is an advocate for, and commentator on, children's rights. He worked at the Children's Legal Centre from 1982 to 1988, and is the father of two young children.